TRUE

DEDICATION

I dedicate this book to Diane Patry – a friend who
made a significant difference.

TRUE

ANDY ECONOMIDES

WORD PUBLISHING

WORD ENTERTAINMENT LTD
Milton Keynes, England

TRUE

First published 2001 by Word Publishing,
9 Holdom Avenue, Bletchley, Milton Keynes, Bucks,
MK1 1QR, UK.

ISBN 1-86024-235-9

Book design and production for Word Publishing by
Bookprint Creative Services, P.O. Box 827, BN21 3YJ, England.
Printed in Great Britain.

CONTENTS

ACKNOWLEDGEMENTS

First and foremost my heartfelt thanks to my wife Annette for your love and our togetherness in Christ. You are my helpmate and dearest friend. I love you. To my daughter Hannah – I am proud of you.

To Soteria Associates – Phil Dowding, Don Egan and Ian Wilson – for your brotherly friendship and partnership in the greatest adventure on earth.

I would like to acknowledge the faithfulness and assistance of my trustees, Robin Kemp, Michael Mellows and Derek Mumford. Also to a real and dear friend since our teenage years, J. John.

Thank you to the Revd Samuel Folahan, respected by others, respectful of others, like a prince among his people.

I would also like to thank Doris Manly, a faithful soldier for Christ, for your encouragement in our work.

A special thank you to the friends and supporters of Soteria Trust who enable us to share the Good News of Christ Jesus in Britain and other countries. You make a difference too.

FOREWORD

Around two thousand years ago a man in his early thirties stood trial in front of one of the most powerful men in the known world. In the course of that exchange a question was posed which has echoed throughout the hearts and souls of countless men and women, rulers and those ruled: 'What is truth?' The irony was that truth was embodied in the person on trial – Jesus Christ.

The job of Christian communicators isn't to paint people wonderful, entrancing new pictures full of new colours and objects. Rather it is to be like ophthalmologists – eye doctors – people who help us see clearly what is already there. Andy works skilfully, standing Jesus in front of us, and confronting us with truth. He works on our eyes so we can see him in sharper, clearer, more transforming focus. Andy communicated the truth about Jesus to me personally when we were students in London in 1975; it completely changed my life.

If you are a Christian this book will refresh your soul by showing you Jesus Christ again. If you have never seen Jesus Christ clearly, you will see him in these pages standing before you. And when our tired, unseeing eyes are opened to glimpse him, he is indeed the most beautiful sight for sore eyes.

With Jesus firmly in focus we are able to see the way ahead, and Andy helps us see the pitfalls and hazards, the routes to the mountain tops and the high places. He gives us essential tools for the journey and writes in such a way that we want to run with him to keep up with God our Creator. And the most important thing about all that he writes is that Andy Economides lives it. I commend to you the man and the book.

J. John

1.

THE SAVIOUR OF THE WORLD

A day that changed his world

Maximilian Kolbe, with four of his companions, was deported to Auschwitz, Poland. Auschwitz was a labour and death camp. Few who passed through the prison gate left the camp alive. Cruelly the prisoners were told that the only way out was through the chimneys of the crematorium. Father Maximilian Kolbe, a Christian minister, received the striped convict garment and was tattooed with the number 16670. He began work immediately, carrying blocks of stone for the construction of a crematorium wall.

Prison law stated that if anyone attempted to escape, ten men from the same bunker would be chosen for death by starvation in the dreaded windowless underground cell. Towards the end of July a prisoner apparently escaped and the men from Kolbe's bunker were led out into the blazing midday sun knowing what to expect.

One man from each line was selected at random, including Sergeant Francis Gajowniczek. The sergeant cried out, 'My wife and children! I shall never see them again!' A man stepped out from the rows and offered to take his place. It was prisoner 16670, Maximilian Kolbe. A German officer asked Kolbe who he was. Kolbe responded, 'I am a Catholic priest. I wish to die for that man. I am old. He has a wife and children.' So it was that Maximilian Kolbe and the nine others were taken to the death chamber of cell 18. Francis Gajowniczek was set free. It was a day that changed his world.

During the next two weeks the prisoners in the death chamber were not given any food or water. One after another they died until only four were left, including Maximilian. The authorities felt that death by starvation was taking too long, and the cell was needed for new victims. Each remaining prisoner was given a lethal injection of carbolic acid (phenol) in the vein of his left arm. Maximilian, with a prayer on his lips, gave his arm to his executioner. Maximilian Kolbe was 47 years old when he was executed.

Maximilian's gift of his life reminds me of Jesus Christ's gift of his life for the whole of humanity.

Three years ago during a trip to Poland I visited Auschwitz, which is still surrounded by a triple row of fences which were originally electrified. Inside the prison chamber I stood motionless, gazing through the bars at the dark and gloomy cell in which Kolbe was kept before his death. I could not but think about the amazing love that this one man had for another. Maximilian's act of love was to sacrifice his own life; it was voluntary. This death had purpose – it allowed another, Francis Gajowniczek, to live to a very old age. Maximilian's gift of his life reminds me of Jesus Christ's gift of his life for the whole of humanity.

The day that changed the world

Two thousand years ago something wonderful happened that would affect the world for ever. It was a day that changed the world. Indeed, it was a day that changed history. It was the day God's Son died. God so loved the world that he gave up his one and only Son to be crucified on the cross so that whoever believes in Jesus today may live abundantly – in this life and in eternity. Since the day Christ died 2000 years ago until today – and for ever – the cross has never lost its power and effect to forgive, bless, empower and grant eternal life through faith.

Jesus Christ took away our sins and sorrows. His death brings us peace of mind and peace with God.

It is important to say that the blood of Jesus is not first and foremost for us; it is for God. Today God looks upon the finished work of his Son and is satisfied that, for everyone who repents, receives and believes, sin has been paid for.

Millions of people through the centuries have discovered this abundant life and peace with God by responding with faith to the old message. These disciples and followers of Christ have become new creations. The new has come and the old has gone and the world is a different and better place. The church celebrates the day on which Jesus died as 'Good Friday'. The only reason that it was a 'good' Friday was that three days later Jesus rose from the dead – on the day we now call 'Easter Day'.

Jesus Christ's act of love was willingly to lay down his life for humanity for all time. We begin our examination of the events that took place by starting at the Garden of Gethsemane the evening before he was crucified. Gethsemane was on the lower slopes of the Mount of Olives just outside Jerusalem, one of Jesus' favourite places.

Overwhelmed with sorrow

Jesus expressed to his dear friends, who had been with him from the beginning of his teaching ministry, his deep distress and trouble. His heart was overwhelmed with sorrow, almost to the point of death. He asked help from his disciples; he needed their friendship, now more than ever. Jesus fell to the ground. He could not help it, because he knew the abuse, suffering, and evil that was to come. He prayed to his heavenly Father, asking that if possible God might take the cup of suffering away from him. But he would rather do God's will, whatever the cost, and therefore acknowledged that he would drink the deadly cup (Mark 14:32–36). While Jesus was talking to his sleepy disciples, Judas the betrayer approached, bringing others with him to arrest Jesus.

Betrayed with a kiss

Judas was aware that people knew Jesus well enough by sight but he felt that in the dim light of the garden they might need a definite indication of who they were to arrest. He chose the most terrible of signs – a kiss. It was customary to greet a rabbi with a kiss; it was a sign of respect and affection for a well-loved teacher. When Judas says, 'The one I kiss is the man,' he uses the word *philein*, which is the ordinary word for kiss. But when it is written that he kissed Jesus, the words used are *kata philein*. The word *kata* indicates intensity. *Kata philein* means to kiss as a lover kisses his beloved. The sign of betrayal was not a mere form of kiss of respectful greeting. It was a lover's kiss. Jesus was betrayed by one of his chosen and closest friends (Mark 14:43–46).

The arresting mob came from the chief priests, the scribes and the elders – the three sections of the Sanhedrin, the Jewish religious council. They marched Jesus away to the high priest. The disciples' nerve cracked. They could not face it. They were afraid that they too would share the fate being prepared for Jesus. They all left him and ran away. But throughout all this Jesus displays serenity, for the struggle in the garden is over, and now there is the peace of a man who knows that he is following the will of God.

Who is Jesus?

The religious trial before Caiaphas, the high priest, was grossly unfair and unlawful. Many people were brought in to tell lies about Jesus, but their statements did not agree and the high priest became exasperated. He asked the question which he knew would get the result he wanted – a sentence of death. '*Are you the Christ, the Son of the Blessed One?*' Jesus answered, '*I am.*' That was it. They condemned him as worthy of death. The issue here was not about any unlawful deed that Jesus may have done. Jesus never did anything that was unlawful or sinful.

They sentenced him to death because of who he claimed to be. He claimed to be the Son of God and the Messiah.

Having passed sentence, they began to spit on him. They blindfolded him and hit him with their fists, taunting him saying, 'Guess who hit you?' The guards also took him and beat him up.

Very early the next morning the chief priests, with the elders, the teachers of the law and the whole Sanhedrin, reached a decision. They bound Jesus, led him away and handed him over to Pilate. He was to be tried by the state now.

Jesus is sentenced to death

Pilate wanted to release Jesus, because he knew that it was out of envy that the chief priests had handed him over. But the continued pressure from the religious leaders and the crowd finally weakened Pilate's resolve to free Jesus. He changed his mind. Now he wanted to satisfy the crowd and he ordered Jesus to be flogged and then crucified.

Roman flogging was a terrible thing. Jesus was stripped naked and tied to the scourging post. The whip had strips of leather studded here and there with pieces of bone and sharpened pieces of lead. The soldiers used this weapon on Christ. His chest, neck, shoulders, back, hips, and legs were slashed as if with knives; his body streamed with blood and was covered with bruises. Even his face was cut and disfigured by the lashes that came down upon him. He was in such a state that he could scarcely have been recognised, even by those who knew him well. Jesus now lay at the foot of the post. A bucket of water mixed with salt was thrown over him, the stinging brine being a routine way to revive a victim and help to stop the flow of blood. Jesus was pulled to his feet and held upright until he could feel some strength return. His body was racked with pain. He stood shivering in shock and struggling to reclothe himself as best he could.

The soldiers then took Jesus into their headquarters and,

calling out the entire company of soldiers, they began to mock him. They dressed him in a purple robe and made a crown of long sharp thorns and rammed it on his head. Then they began to salute him, 'Hail, king of the Jews!'

They beat him on the head with a stick, spat in his face, and dropped to their knees in mock worship. When they were tired of their mocking they took off the purple robe and put his own clothes on him. He was led out to be crucified. The slow walk to Golgotha, the place of the skull, began.

Three soldiers were ordered to complete the execution. The commanding officer took the unusual step of attaching a *centuria*, a further hundred troops in full battle dress, to accompany them. This was a precaution against any attempt to intervene in the proceedings. The procession assembled. First came five rows of soldiers, ten in each row, followed by the execution party made up of three soldiers and Jesus carrying his cross. Then came a further five rows of soldiers, again with ten soldiers in each row. Caiaphas, the high priest, along with the religious guard, walked behind the Roman soldiers and the public followed. There were probably close to 4,000 people who went to see Jesus die. The longest way to the place of execution was taken, passing through the business quarter and shopping area. They followed every possible street and lane so that as many people as possible could see and take warning. Jesus, already badly beaten, stumbled under the weight of the heavy cross. A man from Cyrene, in northern Africa, was close by and they forced him to carry Jesus' cross.

When they reached the place of crucifixion the cross was laid flat on the ground. Jesus was stretched on it and his hands were nailed to the wood. His feet were loosely bound. Between his legs projected a ledge of wood, called a saddle, to take the weight when the cross was raised upright. The cross was then lifted upright and set in its socket. Jesus was left to die. Sometimes prisoners hung for days, suffering hunger and thirst and the terrible struggle to breathe. They offered Jesus drugged wine to ease the pain but he refused it. In the shadow of the cross the soldiers diced for Christ's seamless garment. It was nine o'clock in the morning when they crucified him. Jesus had already suffered so much abuse but it was not over yet. Passers-by ridiculed him. At three o'clock Jesus breathed his last breath. His mission was accomplished (Mark 15:21–39).

... the cross has never lost its power and effect to forgive, bless, empower and grant eternal life through faith.

As evening approached, Joseph of Arimathea, a prominent member of the council, went to Pilate and asked for Jesus' body. Pilate, having received confirmation of Jesus' death, gave permission for Joseph to take the body. Joseph had Jesus' body wrapped in linen and placed in a tomb cut out of rock. A stone was rolled against the entrance of the tomb. Roman soldiers were posted outside the tomb keeping guard. A Roman wax seal was set between the stone door and the entrance. The soldiers had the responsibility to ensure that the seal was not broken. They guarded the seal with their lives, because Roman law for soldiers stated that allowing a seal to be unlawfully broken was punishable by death.

Christ is risen!

Early on the first day of the week, while it was still dark, Mary of Magdala went to the tomb and saw that the stone had been removed from the entrance. So she came running to Simon Peter and the other disciple, the one Jesus loved, and said, 'They have taken the Lord out of the tomb, and we don't know where they have put him!'

So Peter and the other disciple started for the tomb. Both were running, but the other disciple outran Peter and reached the tomb first. He bent over and looked in at the strips of linen lying there but did not go in. Then Simon Peter, who was behind him, arrived and went into the tomb. He saw the strips of linen lying there, as well as the burial cloth that had been around Jesus' head. The cloth was folded up by itself, separate from the linen. Finally the other disciple, who reached the tomb first, also went inside. He saw and believed (John 20:1–8).

One thing is certain: if Jesus had not risen from the dead, we would never have heard of him. The attitude of the women was that they had come to pay their last tribute to a dead man. The attitude of the disciples was that everything had finished in tragedy. By far the best proof of the resurrection is the existence of the Christian church. Nothing else could have changed sad and despairing men and women into people radiant with joy and flaming with courage. The resurrection is the central fact of the whole Christian faith.

The resurrection of Jesus makes Christianity unique

The religious leaders wanted Jesus executed because of who he claimed to be – the Son of God (John 3:16–18). They rightly understood that this claim to be the Son of God meant equality with God. Jesus was claiming to *be* God (John 5:16–19; 10:29–36).

The bodily resurrection of Christ on that first Easter Sunday validates and confirms his claim to be the Son of God. The resurrection also confirms his words and promises to humanity. Jesus spoke of blessings in this life and eternal life in the next. We can be sure of being with God after this life because Jesus promises it, his resurrection makes it believable and possible.

Knowing Jesus means experiencing life to the full in this world and the next. Jesus came for that purpose.

Because we believe in the resurrection something important follows. Jesus is a living presence, not just a person in a book. It is not enough to know the story of Jesus. We may begin that way but we move on to meeting him. The Christian life is not the life of a person who knows about Jesus, but the life of a person who knows him. There is all the difference in the world between knowing about a person and knowing a person. Most people know about the President of the United States of America, but few actually know him. The resurrection of Jesus makes Christianity unique. There is no one like Jesus Christ – he is unequalled, unusual and remarkable. Knowing Jesus means experiencing life to the full in this world and the next. Jesus came for that purpose. Know Jesus – know life! No Jesus – no life!

Jesus' death has purpose

Jesus Christ gave up his life willingly. He allowed his life to be taken. He was in control, although the people responsible for his death thought that they were.

While Jesus hung on the cross he cried out those incredible words, 'It is finished!' He immediately breathed his last, gave up his spirit and died. It was a cry of victory: 'I have done it!' He accomplished his ultimate purpose when visiting our world, that of shedding his blood on the cross for the forgiveness of our sin and to bring us to God. We no longer have to be separated from God who is holy and without sin. Separation means no real communication with God is possible. This separation is like a thick cloud that prevents the warm sun from shining on us. The Bible says:

> Surely the arm of the Lord is not too short to save, nor his ear too dull to hear. But your iniquities have separated you from your God; your sins have hidden his face from you, so that he will not hear (Isaiah 59:1–2).

When our sin is removed the way to God is clear and we can be friends with our heavenly Father. The purpose of Christ's cross is to bring you to God by removing your sin. The cross of Christ has never lost its power and purpose. 'For Christ died for sins once for all, the righteous for the unrighteous, to bring you to God' (1 Peter 3:18).

Christ is the way to God. It was for our sins that Christ died. The good and righteous one died for us so that we could come to God. Being brought to God means living in close friendship with God, meeting him and knowing him. That is eternal life. It is knowing God and Jesus Christ. Not knowing about but actually knowing God and his Son, Jesus (John 17:3).

The prophet Isaiah predicted the coming Messiah, or Christ:

> But he was pierced for our transgressions, he was crushed for our iniquities; the punishment that bought us peace was upon him, and by his wounds we are healed. We all, like sheep, have gone astray, each of us has turned to his own way; and the Lord has laid on him the iniquity of us all (Isaiah 53:5–6).

On the cross Jesus literally took our transgressions on himself. Transgressions means breaking God's laws. We have all done that. He carried our iniquity. Iniquity is the evil that we have done. He was punished that we may have peace. Peace with God. Peace with ourselves. Jesus' death has purpose.

First you need to repent from sin . . . Secondly you must receive Jesus Christ . . . Thirdly you need to believe . . .

You can know forgiveness. You can become a new creation. All of this is done by God. It is his power within your life, transforming the rest of your life, the power being the Holy Spirit coming within you, giving you a spiritual birth. It is being born again by the Holy Spirit.

For this to happen you must do your part and God will certainly do his. First you need to repent from sin, to feel deep sorrow about your sinful actions and resolve not to continue in your old ways that are not according to the teaching of the Bible. This change of mind is a turning from sin and turning to God. If we claim to be without sin, we deceive ourselves, but if we confess our sins to God he is faithful and just and will forgive us our sins and purify us from all unrighteousness

(1 John 1:8–9). The Saviour of the world died to bring forgiveness. Embrace the Saviour. You need him. Jesus' death has purpose.

Secondly, you must receive Jesus Christ, the Son of God.

Some, however, did receive him and believed in him; so he gave them the right to become God's children. They did not become God's children by natural means, that is, by being born as the children of a human father; God himself was their Father (John 1:12–13 Good News Bible).

Receive and believe

Receiving Jesus means to welcome him into your life. He wants to come and live within your life by his Spirit. Jesus stands at the door of your life and knocks, waiting for you to open the door and invite him in. He says:

'Here I am! I stand at the door and knock. If anyone hears my voice and opens the door, I will come in and eat with him, and he with me' (Revelation 3:20).

To receive Jesus means no longer living your life without him. It involves receiving his ways and purposes for your life. Receive him gladly as your Lord and let him have his way.

Thirdly, you need to believe that God so loved the world that he gave his only Son to be crucified for your sins. It also means believing in God's risen Son, Jesus the Saviour. Will you put your trust in the cross of Christ? Will you embrace Christ as your personal Saviour? For those who repent, receive and believe, a miracle happens – they experience the new birth, they are born again.

Think of Jesus knocking now, asking to come into your life. You want him to come in, or perhaps you want to make sure he has come in. It may help you to say this prayer quietly, phrase by phrase, thinking carefully about what you are saying, what you are doing:

Lord Jesus Christ, I know I have sinned in my thoughts, words and actions. There are so many good things I have not done. There are so many wrong things I have done. I am sorry for my sins and turn from everything I know to be wrong. You gave your life on the cross for me. Gratefully, I give my life back to you. I ask you to come into my life. Come in as my Saviour to cleanse me. Come in as my Lord to control me. Come in as my Friend to be with me. And I will serve you all the remaining years of my life in complete obedience. Amen.

Asking Jesus into your life is the first step – like greeting someone you have just met. Getting to know someone well takes time and effort. It is the same with Jesus. We can get to know Jesus better through the Bible, through prayer and through the local church. Most importantly God has given us the Holy Spirit to enable and empower us. The Holy Spirit is a wonderful person available to you, to help you become like Jesus. The Holy Spirit will comfort, strengthen and guide you. Please turn to the chapter on the Holy Spirit for further help.

2.

FOUR STEPS FOR THE NEW CHRISTIAN

There is only one requirement for salvation – faith in Jesus Christ. Just believe in him. That is all you need to do. Have you trusted Christ as your Saviour and Lord? If you have, you have salvation. To enable you to move forward towards spiritual maturity, the Lord has given various things to help you: baptism, the church, prayer and the Bible.

Baptism

Whoever knows Christ as their Saviour and Lord can be baptised. Those who believe and have accepted the message of Christ should be baptised. Baptism and believing go together. There are three good reasons for baptism.

First, we should be baptised in obedience to Jesus Christ. Jesus gave the great commission to the church, instructing them to baptise disciples in the name of the Father, the Son and the Holy Spirit (Matthew 28:18–20).

Another reason for baptism is to prepare us to serve Christ. Jesus' baptism prepared him to serve God and others. At the moment Jesus came up out of the water he saw the Spirit of God descending in the form of a dove and a voice said, 'This is my Son, whom I love; with him I am well pleased' (Matthew 3:16–17). After this experience Jesus went out to preach and heal.

Saul, later called Paul, was also baptised, which prepared him to serve. Paul was dramatically converted to Jesus Christ while on his journey to Damascus. During this experience he lost his sight. When Ananias went to the house where Paul was staying and placed his hands on him, Paul's sight was restored and he was filled with the Holy Spirit, got up and was baptised (Acts 9:1–19). For Jesus and Paul water baptism and being filled with the Holy Spirit came before they began to serve.

We should be baptised in obedience to Jesus Christ ... to prepare us to serve Christ ... to demonstrate our faith in Christ.

The third reason for baptism is to demonstrate our faith in Christ. The person being baptised is identifying themselves as a Christian. The act shows that the person is not ashamed of who they are and their decision to follow Jesus Christ (Mark 8:38).

The meaning of baptism

Baptism is a sign that certain things have happened to the person who has decided to follow Christ. However, it is not only an outward sign of an inner reality. It is an opportunity for God to continue his work of blessing and grace in the life of the believer. At your baptism expect God to fill you with his Spirit and empower you to serve. Expect God to break the power of cancelled sin in areas of your life. In Nigeria I have witnessed people who were baptised in water just days after becoming Christians receiving the baptism in the Holy Spirit and deliverance from evil spirits. Let faith arise for greater things.

First, baptism signifies the washing away of sins. Just as water cleanses our bodies so baptism is a sign that our sins have been washed away from us. Paul was told, 'Now what are you waiting for? Get up, be baptised and wash your sins away, calling on his name' (Acts 22:16). If we confess our sins the blood that Jesus shed on the cross forgives and cleanses us.

Secondly, baptism demonstrates the burying of our old life. During baptism the immersing under the water represents what happens when someone dies and is buried in the ground.

Baptism represents death of the person's old life and ways (Romans 6:4). The old life has gone. When the person is raised from the water it represents new life. Becoming a Christian is about becoming a new creation; the old has gone and the new has come and all this is from God (2 Corinthians 5:17). Baptism shows this.

Thirdly, baptism is a sign of our receiving the Holy Spirit. Peter told the crowd to turn from sin and be baptised and they would receive the Holy Spirit. Jesus and Paul received the Holy Spirit with power at baptism. Expect to receive God's power at baptism. Baptism in water and baptism in the Holy Spirit are sometimes linked in experience and this shows itself in Scripture (1 Corinthians 12:12–13).

And fourthly, baptism is a sign that we have joined the church, the body of Christ. By baptism we are brought into the family of the church. All Christians, whatever nationality and background, should be baptised. Baptism should not be restricted to adults of eighteen years and over. There are those who have not reached adulthood who have believed and received Jesus Christ into their lives. These young people should be baptised.

Early baptism is the biblical way and the church needs to put a higher value on it.

The word 'baptise' means to immerse, plunge or sink. This is why many churches baptise people by completely immersing them in water; baptism was usually done this way in New Testament times and Jesus was baptised this way in the River Jordan. Today people can be baptised in a church building, in a river, the sea, a swimming pool, or anywhere where there is water.

Give baptism priority

New converts and those who have not been baptised should be baptised immediately. Early baptism helps to strengthen and

seal the decision to follow Christ. Early baptism is the biblical
way and the church needs to put a higher value on it. God's
power is released at baptism.

The Ethiopian official had the Good News of Jesus
explained to him by Philip the evangelist (Acts 8:26–40). As
they travelled together and talked, the Ethiopian saw some
water and said, 'Look, here is water. Why shouldn't I be baptised?' He ordered the chariot to stop. Then Philip and the
Ethiopian official went down to the water and Philip baptised
him. We see that when the Ethiopian became a Christian he
wanted to be baptised straight away. What is keeping you from
being baptised? What are you waiting for? Ask your church
leaders to baptise you.

The church

A few weeks after I became a Christian at the age of seven-
teen, Andrew Liversidge came to my home. I knew him
slightly from school days. He had heard that I had become a
committed follower of Jesus Christ and asked if I would like
to join the church youth fellowship that he attended. I am so
glad that he cared enough to follow up my decision to follow
Christ. I started to attend the youth fellowship which met on
Saturday and Sunday evenings. Soon I also went to the
Wednesday evening meeting which met in the youth leader's
home for Bible study, prayer and fellowship. The youth leader,
Roger Stacey, became a spiritual father to me. Those early
years were vital in my formation and development as a
Christian. The love and care that Roger and his wife Kate
gave to me was wonderful. They were true shepherds. Later I
became one of the leaders of the youth fellowship. It was
there that I met a lovely young woman whom I fell in love
with and married. During this time I also attended church
regularly on Sunday mornings and made friends with other
Christians.

I am so glad that he cared enough to follow up my decision to follow Christ.

The Christian needs to attend the fellowship of believers; that is the church. This fellowship is the coming together of people in friendship. In the early church those who heard, believed and accepted the message of Christ spent their time learning from the apostles' teachings, taking part in the fellowship, sharing in the fellowship meals and the prayers (Acts 2:42). The fellowship meals were times when the believers would come together to eat and drink, with an opportunity to remember the death of Christ with bread and wine representing the body and blood of Christ. Today the church has the Communion or the Breaking of Bread service to remember what Jesus did for us on the cross. The church is the community of believers in togetherness and friendship.

The early church continued together in close fellowship and shared their belongings with one another. They would sell property and possessions and give the money to the apostles to distribute among those in the church who were in need (Acts 2:44). The church must be a sharing people who demonstrate practical love for one another.

Prayer

There is power in prayer. The early church devoted themselves to prayer and praise in public places and in their homes (Acts 2:42–47). Prayer is simply speaking and listening to God. Prayer includes praise, thanks and biblical meditation – reading and thinking about the word of God. The Bible is necessary if we are to be thoroughly equipped in life for all situations and good works. God is holy and so prayer includes confession of sin. God is our heavenly Father, once we have believed in and received Jesus into our lives (John 1:12–13). We can tell him about our needs and ask for his help. Prayer includes praying for others. God loves the world and so must we. Often we are prompted not only to pray but to help in practical ways.

The Bible

We receive teaching from the Bible, church meetings and Christians. It is a big advantage to have a healthy and positive attitude when we hear the word of God taught. Make a decision to take home at least a crumb from every meeting.

Read, reflect on and apply the word. Discipline yourself to set aside time to do this. Blessed is the person whose delight is in the word of God and who meditates on it often. That person will become like a tree planted by streams of water which produces fruit at the right time. Its leaves will not dry up. That person will succeed in everything they do (Psalm 1).

New Christians will benefit greatly from reading and reflecting on the accounts of Jesus found in the gospels. Start by reading Mark's Gospel straight through in just a few sittings. Then go back to the beginning and read a small section at a time. Think and reflect. Take your time. Enjoy it. Let it touch your heart. Let it speak. Spend months on this gospel. Ask yourself after each small section, 'What did Jesus say? What did he do?' Look at his compassion. Is there a promise to claim? Allow him to speak to you. Most importantly get to know him more.

Sometimes the most simple thing will bless your heart. To the blind beggar Jesus said, 'What do you want me to do for you?' (Mark 10:46–52). Jesus asks you the same question today. In this story of the healing of blind Bartimaeus these words speak to me more than anything else about the compassion of Christ. Jesus was walking with a large crowd when Bartimaeus cried out. Some of the crowd told Bartimaeus to be quiet but Jesus stopped and said, 'Call him.' Today Jesus stops for you. He won't ignore you or pass you by.

3.

HOW TO LIVE BY THE HOLY SPIRIT

The Holy Spirit is a counsellor, comforter and divine helper. Jesus Christ promised his disciples that they would experience a baptism with the Holy Spirit. Jesus told them he was going away, back to God, but that he would give them the Holy Spirit. Jesus always addressed the Holy Spirit as him or he, never as it (John 14:15–17; 16:5–11).

The Holy Spirit is a very powerful person. He is not a force. The Holy Spirit has personality. He speaks, guides and can be grieved (Ephesians 4:30). Fellowship and friendship with the Holy Spirit are encouraged (Philippians 2:1). Paul concludes his second letter to the church in Corinth by praying this prayer for them: 'May the grace of the Lord Jesus Christ, and the love of God and the fellowship of the Holy Spirit be with you all' (2 Corinthians 13:14).

Jesus told Nicodemus that he must be born again if he was to enter the kingdom of God – born again of the Holy Spirit (John 3:1–8). Jesus explained to Nicodemus that as he had had a physical birth, so he must have a spiritual birth through the Holy Spirit.

The Holy Spirit is the Spirit of truth. The Holy Spirit is the Spirit of Jesus; that is, he is the same in character as Jesus. The Holy Spirit is the third person of the Trinity. There is only one God. God-the-Father, God-the-Son (that is, Jesus), and God-the-Holy Spirit; three distinct persons.

When the Holy Spirit controls the life of the believer he produces these qualities: love, joy, peace, patience, kindness,

goodness, faithfulness, gentleness, and self-control (Galatians
5:22–23). The Holy Spirit gives gifts to Christians as and when
he decides, as we earnestly desire him and have fellowship with
him. He gives wisdom, knowledge, faith, healings, miraculous
powers, prophecy, the ability to distinguish between spirits,
speaking in tongues, and the interpretation of tongues
(1 Corinthians 12:7–10).

The Holy Spirit and Jesus

Jesus was anointed of the Holy Spirit. He was able to heal,
deliver people from evil spirits, do the miraculous, and teach
and preach powerfully, bringing help and relief. Jesus walked
and talked with the Holy Spirit. Jesus did amazing things
because of the Holy Spirit's power in and through him.

'The fellowship of the Holy Spirit be with you.'

John the Baptist appeared in order to prepare the way for
Jesus. John instructed people to repent and get ready for the
coming of the Christ. John baptised those who repented in the
River Jordan. The water signified being cleansed from sin and
new life. John said this of Jesus:

> 'I baptise you with water. But one more powerful than I will come,
> the thongs of whose sandals I am not worthy to untie. He will
> baptise you with the Holy Spirit and with fire' (Luke 3:15–16).

Jesus experienced the tremendous power of the Holy Spirit.
After the resurrection Jesus baptised others with the Holy
Spirit and with fire.

John baptised Jesus in water. While Jesus was praying the
heavens opened and the Holy Spirit came down on him in the
form of a dove. A voice came from heaven that said, 'You are my
Son, whom I love; with you I am well pleased' (Luke 3:21–22).

Jesus returned from the Jordan full of the Holy Spirit. He
was led into the desert by the Holy Spirit. There he was tempted

by the devil for forty days (Luke 4:1–2). Jesus went to Galilee in the power of the Spirit. The whole countryside heard about Jesus. He travelled around, teaching in the synagogues. Everyone praised him (Luke 4:14–19). He went to Nazareth, the town where he had grown up. On the Sabbath he went to the synagogue. The scroll of the prophet Isaiah was handed to him. He carefully unrolled it and found the place where it said:

'The Spirit of the Lord is on me, because he has anointed me to preach good news to the poor. He has sent me to proclaim freedom for the prisoners and recovery of sight for the blind, to release the oppressed, to proclaim the year of the Lord's favour' (Luke 4:17–19).

He rolled up the scroll, gave it back to the attendant and sat down. Everyone looked at him, waiting and wondering. Jesus said to them: 'Today this scripture is fulfilled in your hearing.'

Jesus announced that he was going to fulfil these things. He was going to bring healing, deliverance and salvation. And he did just that. Throughout his life and ministry the Spirit of God was on him. He was anointed by the Holy Spirit. He drove out evil spirits from people (Luke 4:31–37; 8:26–39; 9:37–45; 11:14–28). He healed many (Luke 4:38–40). He healed those with leprosy (Luke 5:12–16). He healed a paralytic (Luke 5:17–26). He healed the centurion's dying servant (Luke 7:1–10). He raised a widow's son back to life (Luke 7:11–17). He raised a dead girl to life and healed a sick woman (Luke 8:40–56). Jesus multiplied a few loaves and fish to feed 5,000 hungry men, plus women and children (Luke 9:10–17). He healed ten lepers (Luke 17:11–19).

Jesus' teaching on the Holy Spirit

One day one of Jesus' disciples asked him if he would teach them how to pray. Jesus taught them the Lord's Prayer. He told them to ask, seek and knock, emphasising that they were to persevere in prayer. To finish he said these words:

'Which of you fathers, if your son asks for a fish, will give him a
snake instead? Or if he asks for an egg, will give him a scorpion? If
you then, though you are evil, know how to give good gifts to your
children, how much more will your Father in heaven give the Holy
Spirit to those who ask him!' (Luke 11:11–13).

Jesus told his disciples that his Father wanted to give the Holy
Spirit – a good gift – to all those who ask. There is no question
whether God will or will not give the Holy Spirit. The
Counsellor, who is our helper and comforter, is available to us.
He will teach us all things and will remind us of the words of
Jesus. He will empower us.

The Holy Spirit comes

After his resurrection Jesus told his disciples to wait in
Jerusalem until the Holy Spirit came on them. He made it clear
that they were not to take the gospel to anyone until they had
received the baptism with the Holy Spirit (Luke 24:45–49; Acts
1:7–8). They waited for the Holy Spirit.

When the Holy Spirit came, it was the Jewish feast of
Pentecost, and the disciples were all together. Suddenly a sound
like a violent wind came from heaven and filled the house. They
saw what seemed to be tongues of fire that separated and came
to rest on each of them. Each of them was baptised or filled
with the Holy Spirit and spoke with other languages or tongues,
as the Spirit enabled them (Acts 2:1–4).

A large crowd had gathered to see what the noise and excitement were about. Peter spoke to them about Jesus. Around
3,000 people heard his message, repented of their sins and were
baptised in water. These new believers joined the church. The
difference that the outpouring of the Holy Spirit made on the
disciples in the upper room was obvious. They now had the
power to witness effectively, just as Jesus had said.

The baptism with the Holy Spirit is given to equip Christians
with boldness and power to share Christ.

The Holy Spirit and me

Immediately after becoming a Christian I attended an excellent youth fellowship. The Saturday sports and games evenings were most enjoyable. The Sunday evening meetings were extremely helpful to me as a young Christian. The speakers, Bible studies, worship and prayer times were instrumental in my formation as a follower of Jesus. I made new friends. Roger and Katie, our youth leaders, became my spiritual parents. They were people I could trust. They helped me to know Christ better.

After attending for six months they organised a holiday in the country for the group. It was a wonderful opportunity to get to know others, have fun and enjoy the Lord's presence. I did not know that something significant was going to happen to me during this time away. The theme of the week was 'The Holy Spirit in the life of the believer'. I asked the guest speakers about the baptism of the Holy Spirit. They suggested I went away and ask God to baptise me with his Holy Spirit. They promised they would pray for me too.

**The joy was so great that I could not sleep ...
That night God baptised me in his Holy Spirit.**

I prayed for the next two days. I remember being apart from the others to pray. I sensed that something was about to happen. I sat on top of a hill praying. As I looked down at the trees, fields and river at the bottom of the hill, I was praying for the baptism with the Holy Spirit. One night we returned to our dormitories to sleep. As I lay on the top bunk I asked God again to give me the baptism with the Holy Spirit and to change me. As I lay praying, joy came pouring into me, a joy that I had never experienced before. I experienced the love of Christ. I felt Christ's love. The joy was so great that I could not sleep. I asked God to take some of the joy away so that I could sleep. I finally fell asleep. That night God baptised me in his Holy Spirit.

The next day I told my youth leaders what had happened. They were delighted. There was an immediate difference in my life. I had an overwhelming desire and ability to share the Good News of Jesus and my story of knowing Christ with others. I shared with friends and strangers. I now had a power and boldness to witness effectively. There were several people that I had known for a long time who became Christians and started to go to church through my witness. I felt the Lord closer to me than ever before. The Bible had greater meaning and was increasingly relevant. I enjoyed praying immensely. For me, Christianity is about knowing Christ and making him known. Since my baptism with the Holy Spirit making him known has been a privilege and challenge.

> 'Every time we say "I believe in the Holy Spirit," we mean that we believe there is a living God able and willing to enter human personality and change it' (J. B. Phillips).[1]

How to be filled with the Holy Spirit

The Lord's desire and plan for you is to baptise you in his Holy Spirit; that is to completely immerse you in his Holy Spirit. Jesus is the baptiser (John 1:33) and he is with you right now. The Holy Spirit is a holy being. The Holy Spirit will not settle in a sinful life. He is sensitive. Heavenly waters will not flow through polluted channels. So it is necessary for you to take the first step and confess and turn away from any wrong doing. We see that in the early church the Holy Spirit was given to those who obeyed him (Acts 5:32).

You do not need to persuade Jesus to be kind to you and baptise you with his Holy Spirit and fire. He has already promised.

Secondly, you must ask. Jesus said the Holy Spirit is given easily to those who simply ask (Luke 11:13). Jesus described the

Holy Spirit to the woman at the well as living water and invited her to ask for this gift of God (John 4:10). Will you ask?

The last step is to believe in Christ and his promise when he says,

> 'If anyone is thirsty, let him come to me and drink. Whoever believes in me, as the Scripture has said, streams of living water will flow from within him' (John 7:37).

By this he meant the Holy Spirit who is available to you today. To come to Jesus begging and pleading is not necessary. Faith involves taking. It is a gift – take it. You do not need to persuade Jesus to be kind to you and baptise you with his Holy Spirit and fire. He has already promised. Come with boldness to collect what he offers you. It is a gift, so you must believe the giver, before you reach out to receive what he offers you.

God offers his Holy Spirit to all. On the day of Pentecost Peter said:

> 'The promise is for you and your children and for all who are far off – for all whom the Lord our God will call' (Acts 2:39).

For many people the baptism with the Holy Spirit comes after becoming a Christian (Acts 8:15–16; 19:1–7). For some, conversion and the baptism in the Holy Spirit happen at the same time.

You need not wait for a special service. Remember to repent of any wrong ways and confess any sin. Ask and believe now. Find a place where you can pray, or ask a Christian friend to help you to pray a prayer like this:

Lord Jesus, I thank you for dying on the cross for me. I give my life totally to you today. I ask you to forgive my sin . . . (mention particular things). *I renounce completely my involvement in . . .* (let the Holy Spirit bring things to mind). *I ask you now to give me your gift and baptise me with the Holy Spirit. I receive you now, Holy Spirit. Come, Holy Spirit. You are welcome. In the name of Jesus Christ. Amen.*

Spend a little time in quiet prayer, thanking God for his grace and goodness. Open your hands in a gesture of receiving. If you have asked and believed, God will keep his promise. We only receive baptism in the Holy Spirit once, for all time. However, we need to ask God to fill us with his Holy Spirit over and over again, every day, as we face certain situations and tasks. The formula is simple: one baptism, many fillings, constant anointing. The reason God anoints you is because he has other people in mind. This experience will not solve all your problems, but it will add a new dimension of power and joy to your life which you never thought possible. May God bless you abundantly, as you discover for yourself the beauty and grace of the Holy Spirit.

Note

1. Taken from *Quotes & Anecdotes for Preachers & Teachers* compiled by Anthony P. Castle (Kevin Mayhew Publishers), page 415.

4.

HOW TO MAKE A DIFFERENCE

You are unique

There is no one like you. You are one of a kind. You were born an original. There is only one of you and you are unique and special. We seem to be able to believe that God loves us, but not that he likes us. God does like us. We need to accept that he likes us and learn to like ourselves.

When a visiting speaker, Gerald Coates, came to our church one Sunday evening, it turned out to be very special. The praise that evening was especially exuberant. It was truly a celebration. Throughout the evening I was feeling expectant that something would happen. I was praying that Gerald would prophesy the word of the Lord to me. I knew that he had been used in this way before. It was almost as if I knew he would. I was full of hope.

When he finished speaking he pointed to four individuals in turn and spoke an encouraging, comforting and strengthening word to each. He spoke clearly, publicly for all to hear. He spoke to me saying that in the future doors would be open for me to speak internationally. He said that God would use my charismatic personality and gifting. He said that there would be occasions when the gift of prophecy would flow through me. People in church that evening were excited for us. I received the word that Gerald had given. I weighed it up and believed it to be true. I kept it in my heart and waited for it to be fulfilled, trying to meet the conditions attached to it.

The word was from the Lord through one of his servants. Something similar happened in the life of Nathanael:

> When Jesus saw Nathanael approaching, he said of him, 'Here is a true Israelite, in whom there is nothing false.'
>
> 'How do you know me?' Nathanael asked.
>
> Jesus answered, 'I saw you while you were still under the fig-tree before Philip called you.'
>
> Then Nathanael declared, 'Rabbi, you are the Son of God; you are the King of Israel.'
>
> Jesus said, 'You believe because I told you I saw you under the fig-tree. You shall see greater things than that.' He then added, 'I tell you the truth, you shall see heaven open, and the angels of God ascending and descending on the Son of Man' (John 1:47–51).

Three months later I attended the annual evangelists' conference in Swanwick, England. During one meeting we got into small groups to pray together. Our group had just finished, but others were still praying. A woman approached me and quietly said, 'I believe I have a word for you from the Lord. Can I tell you it?' At once I recognised her voice and knew her to be Jean Darnall. The essence of what she said was this:

> I see you with a microphone in one hand and a notebook in the other. From your notebook you are preaching other people's words and sermons. Put the notebook away. You are unique and original. Again, I see you on a platform with your Bible in one hand and a microphone in the other. You are speaking powerfully God's word from the Bible to thousands. You are unique and original. Be so.

Somehow, by the gift of the Holy Spirit given to her, Jean Darnall knew something of my past, what I was like, and predicted something about my future. Concerning the future – it came true. It was true that I had been using other preachers' sermons. The emphasis on being unique and original was helpful and challenging for my formation. The part about speaking to large crowds with only my Bible and a microphone was to be fulfilled sooner than I knew.

A few weeks afterwards, Korky Davey, a wonderful evangelist and facilitator of others, had invited me to be part of his team on a trip to Nigeria. This was the most amazing and challenging time of my life. On the first Sunday of our trip, we were seated with the other leaders at the front of the church. There were thousands of people in front of us. Korky turned quietly and informed me that I was to speak. I was not prepared. Many thoughts rushed through my mind. My little sermon outline book was with me. I spoke to the best of my ability but I felt hindered, not liberated. I was not entirely happy. Why? I was tied down to notes. I had not learnt to be myself – unique and original as Jean Darnall had said.

**There is no one like you. You are one of a kind.
You were born an original.**

For the first few days I took the little sermon outline book with me, but it did not help. The word given to me by Jean Darnall was for now and it came to mind vividly. I made the decision to leave behind the outline book. It was time to be original and unique, to depend on God and myself.

Each time I was asked to preach I spoke with only my Bible in hand. I spoke with passion from my heart. This was a new beginning for me. There would be more visits to other nations in Africa and Europe. On every occasion I would speak with the Bible in hand. I had learnt a valuable lesson; God has made me unique and original. There is no need to try and be someone else. The textbook definition of preaching is: 'God speaking through personality.'

You too are unique. We are born original but the majority of people die as copies. With the gifts that God gives you, you can make a difference to your family, your friends, your church, and the world.

You are talented

There was a certain man about to go on a journey (see Matthew 25:14–30). He called his servants and put them in charge of his property. He gave to each one according to his ability. One servant received five talents, another two and another one. This parable that Jesus told has vital lessons for us today.

A 'talent' was a unit of coinage. One talent was the same as 1,000 gold coins. The talents were entrusted to the three servants and it was their responsibility and opportunity to make money for their master. The servant who had five talents put his money to work and earned five more. Similarly the servant who had two talents earned two more. But the servant who had been given one talent dug a hole in the ground and hid it.

After a long time the master returned and settled accounts with them. He congratulated the first two servants and rewarded them with gifts because of their faithfulness in managing what they had been given. The servant who was given one talent tried to justify himself by saying, 'Master, I knew that you are a hard man, harvesting where you have not sown and gathering where you have not scattered seed. So I was afraid and went out and hid your talent in the ground. See, here is what belongs to you.'

The master was not pleased with this and told his servant that he was lazy and bad. He asked him why he did not put the talent to some use by placing it in the bank to earn interest. The one talent was removed from the servant and given to the one who had ten. Jesus concluded the parable by saying:

> 'For everyone who has will be given more, and he will have an abundance. Whoever does not have, even what he has will be taken from him. And throw that worthless servant outside, into darkness, where there will be weeping and gnashing of teeth' (Matthew 25:29–30).

There are three important principles to note here.

1. Each and every Christian is given a gift. Jesus uses the term talent to indicate an ability or gift given to an individual. God has given us time, gifts and other resources. He expects us to put them to good use. No one is excluded. Jesus, like the master in the parable, is wise and discerning to know what to give. No

Christian receives more or less than he or she can handle. If we fail in our task our excuse cannot be that we are overwhelmed. The lack of success may be because of laziness or disobedience.

2. Fear can stop us. The servant said to the master, 'So I was afraid and went out and hid your talent in the ground' (Matthew 25:25). Fear prevented the servant using the talent he was given. He was obsessed with safety and security. Do not bury your talent. Use your God-given gifts to advance the kingdom of God and to do good. Do not be afraid. Many Christians have stopped using or never started to use their gifts or talents. Our time, ability or money is not ours – we are care-takers not owners. Christians must not ignore, squander or abuse what they have; inaction for whatever reason is inappropriate. 'Iron rusts from disuse, stagnant water loses its purity, and in cold weather becomes frozen. Even so does inaction sap the vigours of the mind.'[1]

The tragedy of life is not being limited to one talent but failing to use the one talent.

---

3. A wrong view of someone or something can hinder us. The servant had a wrong view of and relationship with his master. 'Master, I knew that you are a hard man . . .' (Matthew 25:24). This perception, together with his fear, prevented the servant from using his talent. There are those who have a poor and inadequate relationship with God. This does not have to be. For Christians God is Abba – Father. He is compassionate and loving towards his children. The kind of fear we should have of God is one of respect and honour, not a dreadful terrifying fear. The servant would have done better if his beliefs and relationship with his master were like that described below:

The Lord is compassionate and gracious, slow to anger, abounding in love. He will not always accuse, nor will he harbour his anger for ever; he does not treat us as our sins deserve or repay us according to our iniquities. For as high as the heavens are above the earth, so great is his love for those who fear him (Psalm 103:8–11).

Whether you are a five-, two- or one-talent person does not matter. You are gifted. The tragedy of life is not being limited to one talent but failing to use the one talent. You can make a difference.

Spiritual gifts

Jesus operated in the power of the Holy Spirit. He was endowed with spiritual gifts. The four gospels clearly show that his three years of public ministry included healings, miracles, deliverance, and prophecy. Many people were set free and given a new start because of the manifestation of the Holy Spirit working through him. The apostle Paul was also able to heal and save because he allowed the spiritual gifts to flow through him. Paul encouraged believers to do the same in order that the church would be built up and made stronger. Paul instructed the church at Corinth to follow the way of love and eagerly desire the spiritual gifts (see 1 Corinthians 12:31; 14:1).

For the good of all

There are different kinds of gifts. There are gifts of wisdom, knowledge, faith, healing, miracles, prophecy, discernment or distinguishing between spirits, speaking in different kinds of tongues, and the interpretation of tongues (1 Corinthians 12:8–10). The Holy Spirit gives these spiritual gifts to each one, as he determines, for the common good (1 Corinthians 12:4–7).

You can make a difference.

Believers must pursue the way of love and eagerly desire the spiritual gifts if these manifestations are to occur in us and through us to others. Paul says to the Christians in Corinth, 'Since you are eager to have spiritual gifts, try to excel in gifts that build up the church' (1 Corinthians 14:12).

Again and again Paul spells out that the edification, strengthening and encouragement of the church is of great importance in the exercise of the spiritual gifts (1 Corinthians 14:4–5; 12–17; 26–31).

In addition to these gifts of the Holy Spirit there are the gifts of Christ. Apostles, prophets, evangelists, pastors and teachers exist to equip the church for service and to build up the church (Ephesians 4:11–13).

The seven gifts of God are listed by Paul: prophecy, serving, teaching, encouraging, giving (to the need of others), leadership, and showing mercy (Romans 12:6–8).

Indispensable people

Paul likens the church to the human body. The church has many parts, with Christ as its head. The body is not made up of only one part, but of many parts.

There are Christians who despise themselves. They say that they do not belong to the rest of the church – the body of believers – because they are not like somebody else: 'Because I am not a hand I do not belong to the body' (1 Corinthians 12:15).

This is unnecessary and unhelpful. It is self-persecution. Unfortunately there are also those within the church who reject their brothers or sisters by saying they are not needed: 'The eye cannot say to the hand, "I don't need you!"' (1 Corinthians 12:21).

I have heard it said that no one is indispensable. That is a myth because the Bible says the opposite. Paul dispels the myth and puts the record straight when he says, 'On the contrary, those parts of the body that seem to be weaker are indispensable' (1 Corinthians 12:22).

There are those in churches who are of paramount importance. Do not be surprised that these are the weaker members.

They are important to God, his church and his kingdom. We cannot do without the weaker members. They are indispensable. The Bible says so. Paul goes on to say that the parts that we think are less honourable or not worth much we should treat with special honour. The parts that are unpresentable or obscure should be treated with special modesty.

You are gifted. What is your gift and contribution? You can make a difference.

Christian giving

The early church was a caring and sharing community. The church in Jerusalem was over 3,000 strong. The Christians spent their time learning from the apostles and taking part in the fellowship. They shared meals and broke bread, remembering the death of Christ. They were committed to prayer and to each other. The apostles performed miracles and wonders in the name of Jesus by the power of the Holy Spirit. The believers continued together in close fellowship and shared their belongings: 'selling their possessions and goods, they gave to anyone as he had need' (Acts 2:45).

As time went on the church continued to be a loving fellowship. The believers were of one heart and mind. The Christians did not claim that their possessions were their own to hold on to, but they shared with anyone who had need. There were no needy people in the church because from time to time those who owned fields or houses would sell them and donate the money from the sale to the apostles. This was then distributed to each according to their need (Acts 4:32–35). This amazing behaviour was voluntary. It did not involve all private property, only that which was needed. It was not a condition of membership into the church.

It is our responsibility and privilege to help those who are destitute, poor or needy.

What we give is very much up to us. There is great need in the world and the church. God has a bias towards the poor and needy. It is our responsibility and privilege to help those who are destitute, poor or needy. The early church was extremely generous. We also need to have open hearts and pockets to do whatever we can.

Paul's words to the Christians in the early church concerning giving are helpful guidance for us today. He encouraged generous giving within their means, for he did not want those who gave to place themselves in distress.

> . . . Give whatever you can according to what you have. If you are really eager to give, it isn't important how much you are able to give. God wants you to give what you have, not what you don't have. Of course, I don't mean you should give so much that you suffer from having too little. I only mean that there should be some equality (2 Corinthians 8:11–13, New Living Translation).

We must be open to the Lord and what he would say to us. A man stood up in a Christian meeting in London and publicly said that he was going to stop his monthly giving to the leisure club and give instead to the needs of his people in Nigeria. This man was faithful to his word and has since helped to sponsor many needy children through school in Africa.

A few weeks after I had preached at one church, our organisation received a generous cheque from a dear elderly woman who said the Lord told her to give it.

While in Africa I felt I should give a donation to all the staff at a Christian college, knowing that doing so would mean that our organisation would not have sufficient funds to pay my salary on time that month. We must let our hearts be touched.

As a family we give each month to our local church and to a full-time evangelist. We also support causes and individuals from time to time.

I have seen great poverty in Africa. Despite this the Christians there give generously. For them giving to God's work is as important as worshipping God – it is part of their worship.

Several collections in one meeting are common. There is joy on their faces as they give. In such places revival has occurred and continues. Let us be generous.

Note

1. Taken from *Quotes & Anecdotes for Preachers & Teachers* compiled by Anthony P. Castle (Kevin Mayhew Publishers), page 110.

5.

HOW TO WIN BY FAITH

To have faith is to be certain of the things we hope for, to be sure of the things we cannot see. No one can please God without faith. Whoever comes to God must have faith that he exists. He rewards those who seek him (Hebrews 11:1–2, 6).

The Bible tells us that it is a person's faith that wins God's approval. We understand that faith matters, to us and to God. Our faith affects those around us. It affects the situations we encounter.

For some people talking about faith brings despair to their hearts. They know a certain level or quality of faith is required but they cannot reach it. They wrongly think that their prayers are feeble, that God is not pleased with their level of faith. Some struggle with faith because they find trusting difficult. Others are suspicious and doubtful. Some feel that God has let them down, so to trust him for a better day is difficult. This feeling that God has let them down affects their demcanour and their walk as a Christian. It can affect everything.

When I preach in Africa one thing becomes very clear: faith seems to fill the air. You can see faith written on the hearts and minds of people. They listen to the messages with expectancy. Anything could happen and it often does. There the church really does believe that Jesus is the same yesterday, today and for ever as the Bible states in Hebrews 13:8. They have faith because they believe that healings and miracles occur. Sadly the same is not true in Britain. Most of us are cursed with a sense of the impossible and that is precisely why miracles do not happen. It seems to me that those who regard themselves as having a weak trust in God do themselves an enormous injury. They disqualify themselves when God does not. Jesus said, '. . . whoever comes to me, I will never drive away' (John 6:37).

Faith cries out

One day a man came to Jesus with faith that was very feeble and weak. However, he cried out for mercy with all the faith that he could and Jesus granted his request (Mark 9:14–29). The man had first brought his son to the disciples to be healed. They tried to heal the boy but could not. An argument broke out between the disciples and the teachers of the law over the lack of healing. When Jesus came on the scene the situation began to change. The father of the boy explained to Jesus that the disciples were ineffective in driving the evil spirit out of his son. Jesus asked the father how long the boy had suffered.

> 'From childhood,' he answered. 'It has often thrown him into fire or water to kill him. But if you can do anything, take pity on us and help us.'
> ' "If you can"?' said Jesus. 'Everything is possible for the person who has faith.'

Jesus stated the conditions needed for the miracle. It was as if Jesus said, 'The boy's cure depends not on me, but on you.' The father could hardly cope with this demand of faith. In anguish he cried out to Jesus, 'I do have faith, but not enough. Help me have more.' Was that good enough for Jesus? Did he accept the faith of the father even though it was inadequate and weak? The answer is a definite yes, even though the prayer, 'Help us, if you possibly can', was most feeble. The father was helpless. Jesus was not going to turn him away. He came to Jesus and asked for help. His faith was faltering, but Christ accepted the father and healed the boy.

It is a shame that Christians rule themselves out when Christ would not do so.

This is the most important aspect of prayer; important because it gives boldness in our approach even when our faith is weak. Jesus receives those who come, however faltering or helpless. Those coming in such condition are not a problem to him. He does not reject those with an apparent lack of faith. A lack of faith or being helpless is only a problem to us. It hinders us, but it should not. It is a shame that Christians rule themselves out when Christ would not do so. A Christian's helplessness is what gets him or her heard by the living Lord Jesus. Helplessness qualifies us in the eyes of Christ.

Winning faith

Victory is won by means of our faith. Those who believe in Jesus, the Son of God, can defeat the world and everything it throws at them. Sometimes what we might regard as defeat is in fact a victory in God's eyes. Even Christians consider death to be a defeat. The death of a respected Christian leader is viewed as a tragedy. We tend to look at suffering as unacceptable. We say, 'Surely this can't be God's plan for us.'

There is a list of heroes mentioned in the book of Hebrews who, through faith, got the victory (Hebrews 11:32–35). They won. They fought and won, shut the mouths of lions, put out fierce fires, escaped being killed by the sword, and received their dead relatives back to life. There were other godly people who appear to have lost and been defeated, until you read what God thought about it. For God, it was victory.

Others, refusing to accept freedom, died under torture in order to be raised to a better life. Some were mocked and whipped, and others were put in chains and taken off to prison. They were stoned, they were sawn in two, they were killed by the sword. They went around clothed in skins of sheep or goats – poor, persecuted, and ill-treated. The world was not good enough for them! They wandered like refugees in the deserts and hills, living in caves and holes in the ground (Hebrews 11:35b–38, Good News Bible).

All those mentioned won by faith, even those who died or who suffered terribly. There are no losers on God's side. We must understand that apparent defeat is often not defeat at all.

What a record all of these have won by their faith! Yet they did not receive what God had promised, because God had decided on an even better plan for us. His purpose was that only in company with us would they be made perfect (Hebrews 11:39–40, Good News Bible).

Being faithful is costly. It cost Abraham the willingness to give up his only son. It cost Esther the risk of her life. It cost Daniel being cast into the lions' den. It cost Stephen death by stoning. It cost Peter a martyr's death. It cost Paul his life. Does it cost you and me anything to be faithful to our Lord?

Leap of faith

God speaks to his people in many different ways. We are familiar with some of them: through the Bible, people, circumstances, the Holy Spirit, dreams or visions, and nature. Often he tells us something that is contrary to our thinking. He sometimes asks us to do something for him or for others that may come as a surprise. He is the God of surprises. As we journey through life we must always be ready to hear and obey. As the old hymn says:

> Trust and obey!
> For there's no other way
> To be happy in Jesus
> But to trust and obey.

Have faith in God. Obey the prompting of the Holy Spirit. Whatever he tells you to do, do it.

One of the biggest leaps of faith that I have ever taken happened while I was on a preaching visit to Nigeria. While I was seated on the platform with my colleagues from England, I knew I had to make a decision to step out of my comfort zone. It was a decision made under the direction of the Holy Spirit.

In front of me were many hundreds of Nigerian Christians at Christ Apostolic Church, Agbala Itura (Vineyard of Comfort), Ibadan. It was a hot spring evening. I felt a boldness welling up inside. My faith in God was strong. It was a daring faith. The kind that puts you on the line. The congregation was expectant for miracles. When I had finished the message I called people forward with specific illnesses. Hundreds came forward. The British team with the Nigerian church leaders went out to these people, laying hands on many and praying for healing. A woman caught my eye. I went over to her and continued to pray for her until I felt she was healed. Something came out of her body. Another person I prayed for was finally delivered from evil spirits at the end of a loud, intense prayer time. People came forward and shared how they had been healed and delivered during the prayer time.

God speaks.

Another time a young evangelist named Joseph was ill. The Lord told me what to do. I telephoned and told Joseph I was sending a handkerchief that he was to place under his pillow for three nights. He did this and was healed.

Happy is the person who does not lose faith

One person with commitment, persistence and endurance will accomplish more than a thousand with interest alone. If you look at the life of anyone who has ever done anything significant they have had more than interest alone. They have had persistence. Jesus said, 'Happy is the man who does not lose faith in me.'

Civil rights leader Martin Luther King inspired and sustained the struggle for freedom, non-violence and social justice in America. He was totally committed to his cause. He endured hatred and extreme opposition. His persistent courage accomplished historical and significant changes. He, with others, brought greater equality and freedom to African Americans. He persevered. Nothing could stop him. But on 4th April 1968, Dr King was assassinated by a sniper as he stood talking on the balcony of his second floor room at the Lorraine Hotel, Memphis. He died in hospital from a gun shot wound to the neck. His passion and principles inspired thousands to continue to work for equality and justice after his death. Even death could not stop the cause.

Nelson Mandela, who was the South African President, was instrumental in breaking down the apartheid system. In an attempt to stop his work, he was imprisoned for sixteen years. But he continued to inspire others from his prison cell. He persevered. Soon after his release from prison in 1990, government rule was given to the black majority and the system which had divided and destroyed lives was at last broken. The healing process has begun for South Africa. Nelson Mandela had an unusual mixture of courage, tolerance, forgiveness, and persistence.

Fix your eyes

Christ was committed. He persisted. During his life and the three years of ministry, he endured hardship and hunger. He endured people forsaking him. He endured the cross. He was committed to the world.

If we are going to do anything significant, be successful and bear much fruit we need to develop the habit of being persistent. According to Winston Churchill, a past British Prime Minister, the nose of the bulldog is slanted backwards so he can continue to breathe without letting go. Whatever you do, do not let go. Do not lose faith. Fix your eyes on Jesus.

Now obviously we should not want to be persistent in something we should be letting go of. I have known people who are determined and very committed to doing something that they should not even be going near. Lawrence Sterne made the distinction: 'Tis known as perseverance in a good cause and obstinacy in a bad one.'[1]

There are occasions when we may be involved in something that is good, but God wants us to do something else. We need wisdom.

Perseverance has its rewards

Therefore, since we are surrounded by such a great cloud of witnesses, let us throw off everything that hinders and the sin that so easily entangles, and let us run with perseverance the race marked out for us. Let us fix our eyes on Jesus, the author and perfecter of our faith, who for the joy set before him endured the cross, scorning its shame and sat down at the right hand of the throne of God (Hebrews 12:1–2).

Run with perseverance. Throw away all that hinders and entangles. In prayer we need to be asking, seeking and knocking. Jesus urges:

'Ask and it will be given to you; seek and you will find; knock and the door will be opened to you. For everyone who asks receives; he who seeks finds; and to him who knocks, the door will be opened' (Matthew 7:7–8).

Keep asking, keep seeking, keep knocking

I remember a remarkable student who was rewarded for her persistence. She was a female student at Prospect College, Ibadan in southern Nigeria. During an assembly where several hundred students were present, the Revd Samuel Folahan, Principal of the college, awarded several grants to enable some of the poorer students to have their fees paid.

It is important for us to be steadfast.

Once this was finished everyone thought that the assembly was almost over. However, this one female student got up out of her seat and walked to the front. All of the other students remained seated. She looked at the Principal. She quietly and politely asked for a grant. The Principal stood firm and said that no further grants would be given that morning. She continued to stand. She did not move. He dismissed her and told her that she could not have a grant. She would not go. She would not take 'no' for an answer. Some of her student friends pleaded with him to give her a grant. They continued to ask patiently. It lasted for several minutes. He finally gave in and rewarded her boldness with a grant. It is so important for us to be steadfast.

On one occasion, when I was preaching at a gospel meeting in Africa where several thousands were gathered, hundreds came forward for prayer. As I began praying for one particular woman I felt that she needed deliverance from evil spirits. I told the evil spirits to go in the name of Jesus Christ. I knew that she was being set free. I persisted and kept on praying. I looked at her and asked God, 'What is happening here? Are the evil spirits gone now? Is she free?' I felt the Lord say to me, 'No, carry on praying.' I continued in prayer on her behalf. She was quiet, seemingly at peace and free. I thought for a moment that the work was finished, but it was not, so I continued until she was completely liberated. During the testimony time she came to the platform and shared how she had been delivered and set free that evening. If I had stopped praying too soon, it would not have happened. Persistence in prayer is the key.

Starting all over again

The famous scientist Sir Isaac Newton owned a dog called Diamond. Diamond did him a very bad turn. Newton had taken eight whole years to write a very important book. One morning he came into his room and found that Diamond had knocked over a candle and the candle had set fire to the book on his desk. Think what that meant: eight whole years of work burnt up. But he could not be angry with a dog that did not know what it was doing. Newton said, 'Diamond, little do you know the labour and trouble to which you have put your master.' He did not look upon that great work as lost for ever, as most people would have done, but sat down at his desk to start all over again.

All of us face trials of some kind. Trials test the quality of our faith in God and in his word. Perseverance will develop within us as we trust during difficult times. As we allow this perseverance to finish its work we will become mature and complete, not lacking anything (James 1:2–4).

Run with perseverance, embracing God's calling and vision in your heart. Perseverance is available. Perseverance does not come from our power, yet it is within our power.

Refuse to listen to the threats of your enemy. On his voyage that resulted in the discovery of America, Columbus refused to listen to the threats of his sailors. As day after day no land appeared, the sailors threatened to mutiny and demanded that they turn back. Columbus would not listen and each day entered two words in the ship's log: 'Sailed on'.

The apostle Paul writing to the first-century Christians urged them: '. . . be on the alert with all perseverance' (Ephesians 6:18, New American Standard Bible).

The Race
D. H. Groberg

1. 'Quit! Give up! You're beaten!'
   They shout at me and plead.
   'There's just too much against you now.
   This time you can't succeed!'
   And as I start to hang my head
   In front of failure's face,
   My downward fall is broken by
   The memory of a race.
   And hope refills my weakened will

As I recall that scene;
For just the thought of that short race
Rejuvenates my being.

2. A children's race – young boys, young men;
   How I remember well.
   Excitement, sure! But also fear;
   It wasn't hard to tell.
   They all lined up so full of hope;
   Each thought to win that race.
   Or tie for first, or if not that,
   At least take second place.
   And fathers watched from off the side,
   Each cheering for his son.
   And each boy hoped to show his dad
   That he would be the one.
   The whistle blew and off they went!
   Young hearts and hopes afire.
   To win and be the hero there
   Was each young boy's desire.
   And one boy in particular
   Whose dad was in the crowd,
   Was running near the lead and thought,
   'My dad will be so proud!'
   But as they speeded down the field
   Across a shallow dip,
   The little boy who thought to win
   Lost his step and slipped.
   Trying hard to catch himself
   His hands flew out to brace,
   And mid the laughter of the crowd
   He fell flat on his face.
   So down he fell and with him hope
   He couldn't win it now –
   Embarrassed, sad, he only wished
   To disappear somehow.
   But as he fell his dad stood up
   And showed his anxious face,
   Which to the boy so clearly said:

'Get up and win the race.'
He quickly rose, no damage done.
Behind a bit, that's all –
And ran with all his mind and might
To make up for his fall.
So anxious to restore himself,
To catch up and to win –
His mind went faster than his legs;
He slipped and fell again!
He wished then he had quit before,
With only one disgrace.
'I'm hopeless as a runner now;
I shouldn't try to race.'
But in the laughing crowd he searched
And found his father's face.
That steady look which said again:
'Get up and win the race!'
So up he jumped to try again,
Ten yards behind the last –
'If I'm to gain those yards,' he thought,
'I've got to move real fast.'
Exerting everything he had
He gained eight or ten,
But trying so hard to catch the lead
He slipped and fell again!
Defeat! He lay there silently
A tear dropped from his eye –
'There's no sense running any more;
Three strikes: I'm out! Why try?'
The will to rise had disappeared
All hope had fled away;
So far behind, so error prone;
A loser all the way.
'I've lost, so what's the use?' he thought.
'I'll live with my disgrace.'
But then he thought about his dad,
Who soon he'd have to face.
'Get up,' an echo sounded low.
'Get up and take your place;

You were not meant for failure here.
Get up and win the race.'
'With borrowed will, get up,' it said,
'You haven't lost at all,
For winning is no more than this:
To rise each time you fall.'
So up he rose to run once more,
And with a new commit,
He resolved that win or lose
At least he wouldn't quit.
So far behind the others now,
The most he'd ever been –
Still he gave it all he had
And ran as though to win.
Three times he'd fallen, stumbling;
Three times he rose again;
Too far behind to hope to win
He still ran to the end.
They cheered the winning runner
As he crossed the line first place;
Head high, and proud, and happy;
No falling, no disgrace.
But when the fallen youngster
Crossed the line last place,
The crowd gave him the greater cheer
For finishing the race.
And even though he came in last,
With head bowed low, unproud,
You would have thought he'd won the
Race to listen to the crowd.
And to his dad he sadly said,
'I didn't do so well.'
'To me, you won,' his father said.
'You rose each time you fell.'

3. And now when things seem dark and hard
   And difficult to face,
   The memory of that little boy
   Helps me in my own race.

For all of life is like that race,
With ups and downs and all.
And all you have to do to win,
Is rise each time you fall.
'Quit! Give up! You're beaten!'
They still shout in my face.
But another voice within me says:
'Get up and win the race!'[2]

Notes

1. Taken from *Quotes & Anecdotes for Preachers & Teachers* compiled by Anthony P. Castle (Kevin Mayhew Publishers), page 15.
2. Taken from *Connecting* by Paul D. Stanley & J. Robert Clinton (NavPress), pages 224–229.

6.

SALVATION SO GREAT

We begin to experience salvation from Jesus Christ when he saves us from our sins, but he goes beyond this and saves us from many things, for many things. He lives to save humanity. Jesus came to seek and save the lost. He saves all who come to him. Christ is the great Saviour. He saves us from our sins. He saves us for heaven. He saves us from mediocrity. He saves us from ourselves; for at times we are our worst enemy. He saves us from harmful habits. He saves us from selfishness and hate. He saves us from worry and brings healing and peace into our lives. He gives us direction and purpose. He saves the rich and poor. He saves people from all cultures, countries and backgrounds. He saves men, women and children. He saves the wise, and the ignorant. He provides and protects. He offers salvation full and free.

The saving power of Jesus Christ that we read of in the four gospels is the same today. In this chapter we will look at two men whom Jesus saved.

The rich man who had everything (Luke 19:1–10)

Zacchaeus was wealthy. He worked for the Roman Government as a chief tax collector. He was responsible for the collection of taxes throughout the region. Ordinary tax collectors worked under his authority.

In those days the Roman Empire placed heavy taxes on all the people under their control. The Jewish people were not in favour of taxes, as they went to support a secular government. However, payment was forced upon them.

You are included in the blessings of God.

Jewish tax collectors, like Zacchaeus, chose to work for the Romans. They were considered by Jewish society as traitors. At best Zacchaeus was disliked, at worst hated. He was rejected, an outcast and sinner. Zacchaeus used his position and office to his advantage by unlawfully extracting money to line his pocket.

One day Jesus was passing through Jericho. Zacchaeus wanted to see what Jesus looked like. Zacchaeus had no apparent needs. He had no need of physical healing. He had no question to ask Jesus. He had no request to make of Jesus. He did not need any money. All he wanted to do was to see Jesus.

Zacchaeus was a short person and could not see over the crowd, neither could he get through them. He ran ahead of Jesus and climbed a sycamore tree and waited.

When Jesus reached the tree, he looked up and asked Zacchaeus to come down, for he wanted to spend the day at his home. It was a divine appointment. Zacchaeus came down immediately and welcomed Jesus gladly. The people saw all that happened and said disapprovingly, 'He has gone to be the guest of a "sinner".'

Jesus was well aware of the state of Zacchaeus's life. Jesus wanted to bring him salvation. Zacchaeus noticed what the people were saying and thinking. He stood up and shocked everyone except Jesus by saying,

'Look, Lord! Here and now I give half of my possessions to the poor, and if I have cheated anybody out of anything, I will pay back four times the amount.'

It is almost unbelievable – half of his possessions to the poor! Very few had been willing to do such a thing. No wonder Jesus praised him highly.

'Today salvation has come to this house, because this man, too, is a son of Abraham. For the Son of Man came to seek and save what was lost.'

Although the Jewish people excluded Zacchaeus, Jesus recognised him to be part of society with all its blessings. Jesus put the record straight, effectively saying to Zacchaeus, 'You are included in the blessings of God. Do not be concerned with what they think.' As usual, Jesus did not mind what others thought of what he said and did. He always did what was right. Jesus was himself and the truth mattered to him.

We have in this story an important summary of Jesus' purpose – to bring salvation, eternal life and the kingdom of God. Jesus came to seek and save humanity, which is lost without him.

Zacchaeus changed his lifestyle from the day he met Jesus. He would no longer cheat anyone. He repented – he changed his mind – which affected his actions. Jesus brought salvation to Zacchaeus, a better life in this world and life after death. Jesus forgave him. He accepted Zacchaeus's offer to pay back any money he had cheated from the people.

I have always liked this little man. He was curious and he was open to Jesus. He overcame his shortcoming – his height. He overcame the crowd. Jesus could only help Zacchaeus because Zacchaeus was open to him.

Have you experienced his great salvation? Has Jesus come to your house and brought salvation?

The paralytic (Mark 2:1–12)

Jesus had travelled throughout Galilee preaching in the synagogues and driving out demons. He returned to Capernaum. The news of his coming spread quickly. In Jesus' day life in Palestine was very open. In the morning doors of houses were opened and anyone who wanted to could go in and out. Doors were only shut if a person wished for privacy. In humbler houses there was no entrance hall and the door opened directly on to the street.

Jesus was visiting such a house. In no time at all many gathered to see him. The house was completely full. There was no room left outside the house either. The crowd both inside and outside were now eagerly listening to the words of the Teacher.

While this was happening four men carrying a paralysed friend on a stretcher approached the scene. The crowd prevented them from getting their friend to Jesus. But they were determined and ingenious.

Jesus knows our deepest needs better than we do.

The roof of the house, like most houses at that time, was flat. The roof was often used as a place of rest and quiet, so usually there was an outside staircase leading up to it. The roof itself consisted of flat beams laid across from wall to wall, about one metre apart. The spaces between the beams were filled with brush wood and then packed tight with clay. It was easy to dig out the packing between two of the beams. It would not damage the house and would be easy to repair.

The four men carried their friend up on to the roof. Once there, they dug out an opening and they lowered the paralysed man down directly in front of Jesus' feet. When Jesus saw this faith that laughed at barriers, he must have smiled. He looked at the paralysed man and said, 'Son, your sins are forgiven.'

This may seem an odd way to begin to heal someone, but Jesus had a purpose in forgiving the man's sins before healing him. The paralytic had an obvious outward need, but Jesus first met the man's deeper need for forgiveness. The sin and shame were gone. He was declared free. Forgiveness is man's deepest need and God's highest achievement. There is no condemnation, only love and forgiveness. Jesus knows our deepest needs better than we do.

I was preaching one Sunday morning in southern France through an interpreter. I spoke about Adam and his need.

> The Lord God said, 'It is not good for the man to be alone. I will make a helper suitable for him' (Genesis 2:18).

Adam needed a helper that was suitable for him. Adam had God as a companion and friend, but God was not enough for Adam's needs. The wonderful creation that surrounded Adam was not enough. God was pleased to provide for him what he needed. Eve, a beautiful woman and suitable companion, was given to Adam.

The woman interpreter approached me at the end of the meeting and expressed her relief at what I had said about God not being enough. The realisation that God is not enough could bring a completeness to her life. It was perfectly acceptable and proper to have someone other than God; to have the friendship and love of a man. This young woman was beginning to receive love and acceptance for her deepest need. God was perfectly happy to provide another friendship in her life. This would not conflict with her life with God, and her desire to put Jesus first.

The authentic Jesus of the gospel is concerned about the needs that matter most, our deepest needs. He is not only concerned with our obvious needs.

Some of the teachers of the law, sitting in the house where Jesus was declaring forgiveness to someone, thought,

> 'Why does this fellow talk like that? He's blaspheming! Who can forgive sins but God alone?'

In other words, 'He has no right to say that and do that. Who does he think he is – God?' Jesus knew immediately what they were thinking, and threw out a challenge:

> 'Why are you thinking these things? Which is easier: to say to the paralytic, "Your sins are forgiven," or to say, "Get up, take your mat and walk"?'

Before they could answer (and I do not believe they either could
have or would have, because Jesus did not give them an opportunity), he answered his own question, in his own unique and
amazing way. He commanded the man to get up, take up his
mat and go home. In full view of everyone the man got up and
walked home. Everyone was amazed. None of them had ever
seen anything like this.

There are those who refuse to be helped by others.

Jesus now completed what he wanted to do in the life of this
dear, unfortunate man. He was now healed of his sickness and
forgiven of his sin and shame. He was free. His outward
obvious need for physical healing was met by Jesus. His inner,
deeper need for Christ's forgiveness was also met by Jesus. He
was made whole.

It was a good thing for him that four good friends showed
practical love. Love in action. They carried him. They faced
several obstacles. The large crowd prevented them getting near
Jesus, but they were determined to see the matter through. It
was an unusual thing to do, to climb the stairs and break the
roof. They lowered their friend down using ropes. They were
courageous, determined and above all loving. When the paralysed man was in front of Jesus their job was done. They con-
tributed well in getting their friend to the Healer.

There have been occasions when friends have come to me and
carried me. At times all of us need to be carried by others. There
are those who refuse to allow themselves to be carried, to be
helped by others. It may be because they pride themselves on
getting along on their own. There is a great need in our day for
individuals, groups and churches to be involved in carrying
those who need assistance.

Jesus was pleased to see the faith of all five men. He was
pleased with the commitment and love shown, and rewarded
them.

Life-giving words

The crowds were attracted to Jesus because the words he preached gave life, hope and freedom. His words and his personality were like a magnet drawing people to him. Jesus continually promised things. He invited people to come. No other person in history has ever been able to do the same because there is no other person who could fulfil such offers. He was and is unique. Nothing has changed. This is the Good News. Listen to the life-giving words of Jesus:

'Blessed are the poor in spirit, for theirs is the kingdom of heaven. Blessed are those who mourn, for they will be comforted.

Blessed are the meek, for they will inherit the earth.

Blessed are those who hunger and thirst for righteousness, for they will be filled.

Blessed are the merciful, for they will be shown mercy.

Blessed are the pure in heart, for they will see God' (Matthew 5:3–8).

To the weary Jesus says:

'Come to me, all you who are weary and burdened, and I will give you rest' (Matthew 11:28).

To the thirsty Jesus says:

'If anyone is thirsty, let him come to me and drink. Whoever believes in me, as the Scripture has said, streams of living water will flow from within him.' By this he meant the Spirit, whom those who believed in him were later to receive (John 7:37–38).

To those who want a living friendship with Jesus today, he says:

'Here I am! I stand at the door and knock. If anyone hears my voice and opens the door, I will come in and eat with him, and he with me' (Revelation 3:20).

Jesus spoke on every issue of life that touches humanity. For example, he spoke helpfully and profoundly on murder, adultery, oaths, truthfulness, love for enemies, giving to the needy, prayer, how not to worry, why not to worry and judging others (Matthew 5–7). Jesus spoke about life and death issues. Let the words of the Saviour help you, guide you and empower you. Allow the Spirit of God with the word of God to bless your heart and life.

7.

THE MAN NO ONE LIKED

The book of Mark is the most chronological of the four gospels. The majority of the events concerning the life of Christ are placed in the order they actually occurred. Though the shortest of the four, the gospel of Mark contains the most events. It is action packed. Mark presents a rapid succession of vivid pictures of Jesus in action. His true identity was revealed particularly by what he did, not just by what he said. It is Jesus on the move. It is the gospel about Jesus Christ, the Son of God. This Christ or Messiah, meaning the anointed one, came to seek and save a lost humanity.

In Mark 10:46–52 we have the most illuminating story of Jesus healing blind Bartimaeus. Try to visualise the scene.

Jesus was passing through Jericho and was on his way out of the city. His disciples and a large crowd were with him. Jesus was on his way to the Passover in Jerusalem. The custom at that time was that whenever a distinguished rabbi or teacher was on such a journey he would be surrounded by a large crowd of people, disciples and learners. They would listen to him as he talked and walked. This was one of the most common ways of teaching.

At the northern gate sat a beggar named Bartimaeus, the son of Timaeus. He heard the sound of feet. He asked what was happening and who was passing. They told him it was Jesus. There and then he set up an uproar to attract Jesus' attention. To those listening to Jesus' teaching, the noise was an offence. People tried to silence Bartimaeus.

Jesus was not interested in customs, traditions or human ways when they interfered with the well-being of people.

Many rebuked him and told him to be quiet. The crowd were not interested in, or sympathetic towards, this unfortunate blind beggar by the wayside. No one seemed to like this man. However, Bartimaeus was not going to allow anyone to take from him his chance to escape from his world of darkness. He cried out a second time with such violence that the procession came to a standstill. Jesus stopped and said, 'Call him.' The people called to the blind man, 'Cheer up! On your feet! He is calling you.' He came to Jesus. Jesus stopped to help an individual against the flow of tradition, against the strength of the crowd. Jesus was not interested in customs, traditions or human ways when they interfered with the well-being of people. The crowd were intent on hearing Jesus. Jesus was happy to follow the custom but he was also ready to cast it aside for the sake of a broken life. Jesus was concerned for Bartimaeus – a beggar, blind, despised and rejected. The people would have preferred the blind man to have stopped crying out so that they could listen to Jesus' teaching. Jesus did not allow that to happen. Jesus changed things. The African-American poet and educator, Melvin Tolson, said:

> Since we live in a changing universe, why do people oppose change? If a rock is in the way, the root of a tree will change its direction.[1]

While on a speaking tour of a number of churches in northern Greece, my friend Costas, a pastor of one of the churches, was showing me round a new church that was being built. It was in a very small village. I could hardly believe my eyes. The church was half completed. When completed it would accommodate about three hundred people. Besides the main Sunday meeting area it would have offices, rooms, rest rooms and a large hall. Within the church grounds existed the older church building, currently being used, a pastor's house and further extensive land. The potential was incredible but there was a problem. There was insufficient money to complete the building. Also the church was unable to pay a salary for the pastor. In my naivety I offered one possible solution. I suggested to Costas that a small section of the land with perhaps the older house be sold off by the church. The proceeds could then be used to complete the building and pay the salary for a pastor. Costas said that would not be possible. I was surprised until I was reminded of the fact that Greeks very rarely sell land or houses. It is their way of life. Land and houses are passed on from one generation to the next. I could not understand the difficulty. Surely it would benefit the people of that community to have the church completed? Surely it would be useful to have a pastor appointed? Why do people oppose change?

In the Acts of the Apostles we read that in the early church there were those who owned land and houses. They sold them and gave the proceeds to the apostles. The proceeds were used to meet the needs of the people and community (Acts 4:34–37). Joseph, also called Barnabas, a Levite from Cyprus, sold a field he owned and presented the money to the church for the benefit of the needy.

What do you want me to do for you?

Returning to our story of blind Bartimaeus in Mark 10:47–52, we read:

> When he heard that it was Jesus of Nazareth, he began to shout, 'Jesus, Son of David, have mercy on me!'
>
> Many rebuked him and told him to be quiet, but he shouted all the more, 'Son of David, have mercy on me!'
>
> Jesus stopped and said, 'Call him.'
>
> So they called to the blind man, 'Cheer up! On your feet! He's calling you.'

Throwing his cloak aside, he jumped to his feet and came to Jesus.

'What do you want me to do for you?' Jesus asked him.

The blind man said, 'Rabbi, I want to see.'

'Go,' said Jesus, 'your faith has healed you.' Immediately he received his sight and followed Jesus along the road.

The people who rebuked Bartimaeus and told him to be quiet soon changed their tune. The people were instructed by Jesus to call Bartimaeus. 'Cheer up! On your feet! He's calling you,' they said. Bartimaeus wasted no time. This was his moment. He threw his cloak aside. He jumped to his feet and somehow the blind beggar came to Jesus. Jesus asked him, 'What do you want me to do for you?' The blind man said, 'I want to see.' Jesus said, 'Go, your faith has healed you.' Immediately he received his sight and followed Jesus along the road.

Today Jesus asks those who come to him the same question: 'What do you want me to do for you?' He does that for us because he is the same today as yesterday. He wants to bless us as he blessed Bartimaeus.

Faith is rewarded

We learn from this story that faith receives its rewards. Bartimaeus was healed because he put his faith in Jesus of Nazareth. Bartimaeus had living faith. Let us examine living faith.

First, faith involves coming to Jesus. Bartimaeus came. He was extremely vocal and unashamed. Next we see that faith is asking. Bartimaeus spoke to Jesus saying, 'Jesus, Son of David, have mercy on me!' He knew something of who Jesus really was – the Christ. He not only came to Jesus but now he was asking this anointed one from God for mercy. He called on Jesus. Another important aspect of living faith is persevering. Bartimaeus was healed because he asked again and again. This was persistence on Bartimaeus's part. Nothing would stop his clamour in order to come face to face with Jesus.

This is living faith ... coming, asking, persevering and believing.

He was utterly determined to meet the one person whom he longed to confront with his trouble. In the mind of Bartimaeus there was not just a nebulous, wistful, sentimental wish to see Jesus. It was a desperate desire. It is that desperate desire that gets things done. It was not easy for Bartimaeus to persevere, as he had much against him. He was a poor, blind beggar, despised and rejected by society. But persevere he did. This aspect of faith has its rewards. Within you exists a God-given endurance that will see you through.

King Robert the Bruce of Scotland, pursued after defeat in battle, hid in a lonely cave. He tried to plan the future, but was tempted to despair. He had lost heart and had decided to give up when he caught sight of a spider. The creature was carefully and painstakingly making its way up a slender thread to its web in the corner above. The king watched as it made several unsuccessful attempts, and thought, as it fell back to the bottom again and again, how it typified his own efforts. Then at last the spider made it! The king took courage and persevered and the example of the spider brought its reward.

Lastly, living faith has a belief or trust in the living Jesus. Bartimaeus had this quality. He knew precisely what he wanted – his sight. Too often our admiration for Jesus is a vague attraction. When we go to Jesus, if we are as desperately definite as Bartimaeus, things will happen. Ask specifically what you need from Jesus. This is living faith. It is coming, asking, persevering and believing.

Note

1. Taken from Melvin Tolson, *African-American Wisdom* (A Running Press Miniature Edition), Philadelphia and London, Running Press Book Publishers, 1996, page 71 (www.runningpress.com).

8.

KEYS TO SUCCESS

We all have keys. Keys open many things. Keys can give us access to locks which keep thieves out and our property safe. A small key can open a large door, and there are different keys to open different doors that lead to success.

Obedience

Obedience to God can lead to many blessings. Obedience to God's word can lead to miracles.

The prophet Elijah asked the widow at Zarephath for a little water and some bread (1 Kings 17:7–16). The widow informed the prophet that she only had a tiny amount of oil and flour. She was gathering sticks to make a small meal for her son and herself. She was poor and told Elijah that this would be their last meal before they died of starvation. Elijah told her not to be afraid. He told her to go home and make him a loaf of bread and then a meal for her son and herself. The prophet spoke God's word to the woman:

> 'For this is what the Lord, the God of Israel, says: "The jar of flour will not be used up and the jug of oil will not run dry until the day the Lord gives rain on the land"' (1 Kings 17:14).

The widow did just as Elijah had told her and there was enough food. Obedience led to her miracle.

For the jar of flour was not used up and the jug of oil did not run dry, in keeping with the word of the Lord spoken by Elijah (1 Kings 17:16).

Obedience opens doors to God's care. Moses was leading Israel out of Egypt into the promised land (Exodus 15:22–27). After travelling for three days they arrived at Marah, where the water was bitter and unfit to drink. The people grumbled at Moses saying, 'What are we to drink?' God told Moses to throw a stick into the water and it became fit to drink. Through Moses the Lord made an agreement with Israel:

'If you listen carefully to the voice of the Lord your God and do what is right in his eyes, if you pay attention to his commands and keep all his decrees, I will not bring on you any of the diseases I brought on the Egyptians, for I am the Lord, who heals you' (Exodus 15:26).

Soon after, they arrived at Elim where there were twelve springs and palm trees. They camped there near the water, finding rest and refreshment. God's promise to care for Israel was on the condition of their obedience to his word. If we submit to God he will care for us.

James says that it is important to listen to God's word, but more important to obey it (James 1:22–25). Listening and doing will open doors for us.

Obedience ... will open doors for us.
Disobedience will have the opposite effect ...

Obedience can make us mighty

The Revd David Yonggi Cho pastors one of the largest churches in the world in Seoul, South Korea. The church numbers hundreds of thousands. He puts their church growth down to prayer and obedience. Obedience to God's word opens the door to all kinds of growth.

The Pharisees in Jesus' day were outwardly very religious and obedient but Jesus warned his disciples not to be like them. Outward obedience to the law without the change of heart would not open the door to the kingdom of God.

> 'For I tell you that unless your righteousness surpasses that of the Pharisees and the teachers of the law, you will certainly not enter the kingdom of heaven' (Matthew 5:20).

The Pharisees were happy to obey the laws outwardly without allowing God to change their hearts and attitudes. Outward obedience without the change of heart is inadequate for Christ. Selective obedience is disobedience. Whatever God tells you to do, do it. His will for us is good, pleasing and perfect. Christianity is not 'pick and choose your favourite sweetie'. Obedience is not always easy. There will be times when God will test us, but he will give us grace to find a way through. His grace is sufficient in our weakness. We can find strength to obey.

In the Garden of Gethsemane Jesus needed strength to go all the way to the cross. He needed strength to obey (Matthew 26:37–38). Jesus' strength to obey came from his close friendship with his heavenly Father. Your friendship with your Father in heaven is also your strength. He will help you to obey.

There may be times when we will have to choose between obeying God and obeying other people. The apostles were persecuted for their faith. The religious authorities told them not to spread the name of Jesus. Peter and the other apostles were brought before the Sanhedrin, the religious council. They said to them, 'We must obey God rather than men!' (Acts 5:29).

Obedience is a key that will open doors. Disobedience will have the opposite effect – doors will remain closed.

Confidence

Two qualities are necessary to succeed in sport – ability and confidence. When a professional footballer loses his confidence, his performance deteriorates.

One key to success is confidence. The Christian's confidence starts with what Jesus has already accomplished for each of us. Let the words from the Bible build your confidence:

> Therefore, brothers, since we have confidence to enter the Most Holy Place by the blood of Jesus, by a new and living way opened for us through the curtain, that is, his body, and since we have a great priest over the house of God, let us draw near to God with a sincere heart in full assurance of faith, having our hearts sprinkled to cleanse us from a guilty conscience and having our bodies washed with pure water (Hebrews 10:19–22).

When Jesus died on the cross the curtain in the temple, which separated people from the Holy of Holies – the Presence of God – was torn in two from top to bottom (Matthew 27:51). Jesus tore down the barrier between God and us. We can now have boldness and confidence to approach our heavenly Father in prayer. It is a new and living way. It is the new covenant or agreement that God has made between himself and us. Jesus' death on the cross gives us confidence in prayer. This permeates all areas of our lives.

God believes in you.

Christians can be the most bold and confident people on earth. Be bold, be strong, for the Lord your God is with you. Your confidence is in the finished work of Jesus Christ, the Son of God.

Confidence boosts ability. What we lack in ability is made up through confidence. Let your confidence show when you pray. The Bible tells us that we should be and can be confident. 'Therefore, brothers, since we have confidence . . . let us draw near to God . . .'

In every area of your life – at work, at school, at college, your business, your home, wherever – be confident.

Have confidence in Christ's wonderful saving act. Have confidence in yourself. God has confidence in you. God believes in you.

Confidence is a key to success. Confidence opens doors on earth. Be bold, because the Lord is with you.

Enthusiasm

Nothing great has ever been achieved without enthusiasm. The same is true for the future. Nothing great will be accomplished by any individual or group without enthusiasm.

Enthusiasm comes from the Greek phrase *en theos* and literally means 'in God'. The Oxford dictionary defines enthusiasm as 'ardent or burning zeal'. Zeal means earnestness or fervour in advancing a cause or rendering service.

The founder of Methodism, John Wesley, had the zeal of the Lord. For him it was an attitude and a way of life. He believed that the world was his parish. He had a travelling preaching ministry that included an annual tour of England and twenty visits to both Scotland and Ireland. He covered an estimated 250,000 miles, mostly on horseback, and preached 40,000 sermons. He kept a detailed journal of his tours, wrote commentaries on Scripture and edited classical works.

His ambition was 'to reform the nation and spread scriptural holiness throughout the land'. With godly enthusiasm Wesley preached Christ, changing the lives of thousands of people. He said:

> Do all the good you can, in all the ways you can, in all the places you can, at all the times you can, to all the people you can, as long as ever you can.[1]

Your enthusiasm stirs

The apostle Paul, writing to the Christians at Corinth, was thankful that their enthusiasm had such an amazing effect:

> For I know your eagerness to help, and I have been boasting about it to the Macedonians, telling them that since last year you in Achaia were ready to give; and your enthusiasm has stirred most of them to action (2 Corinthians 9:2).

The enthusiasm of the Christians in Achaia was such that it
stirred up the churches in Philippi, Thessalonica and Berea to
give financially and sacrificially to help the impoverished believers in Jerusalem. Paul was now asking the Corinthian church to
complete the collection that they had begun as it had apparently
slowed down or come to a standstill. He took it upon himself to
assist in gathering this collection and to oversee its delivery
through the safe hands of Titus, fellow worker and assistant to
Paul in his missionary work. It was the Corinthians' zeal in
giving that had started and motivated the other collections.
Enthusiasm is infectious. It stirs up others to take action.

As part of my sabbatical I spent ten days at the Christ for all
Nations (CfaN) 'Fire Conference' in Addis Ababa in Ethiopia.
I wanted to learn as much as I could from the evangelist
Reinhard Bonnke, the founder and director of CfaN. Iron
sharpens iron. The purpose of the conference was to equip and
motivate the 10,000 Christians gathered, of whom the majority
were in leadership, in effectively sharing the gospel of Christ.
The wonderful Ethiopians gathered daily to hear Reinhard
Bonnke teach. The reason he spoke so effectively was because
he spoke with enthusiasm and passion. Reinhard is in love with
those he ministers to and so the hearts and lives of the
Ethiopian Christians were stirred for action.

On returning to England I found I was different. My passion
for God increased. His calling on my life as an ambassador for
Christ, proclaiming the Good News, was ignited afresh. I was
fired up.

Do not put out the Spirit's fire (1 Thessalonians 5:19).

Whatever your hands find to do, do it with all your might
(Ecclesiastes 9:10).

Jesus – gentle and zealous

In the temple courts Jesus found some people selling cattle,
sheep and doves; others were sitting at tables exchanging

money. The outer courts were the one place that Gentiles could come to pray and worship. However, these courts had become a noisy, smelly marketplace; the Jewish religious leaders were interfering with the provision God had given to the Gentiles.

What was Jesus' response? John, who was one of Christ's closest disciples, records:

> So he made a whip out of cords, and drove all from the temple area, both sheep and cattle; he scattered the coins of the money changers and overturned their tables. To those who sold doves he said, 'Get these out of here! How dare you turn my Father's house into a market!'
>
> His disciples remembered that it is written, 'Zeal for your house will consume me' (John 2:15–17).

Our Lord Jesus is zealous. Our God is zealous, accomplishing his purposes.

> For to us a child is born, to us a son is given, and the government will be on his shoulders. And he will be called Wonderful Counsellor, Mighty God, Everlasting Father, Prince of Peace. Of the increase of his government and peace there will be no end. He will reign on David's throne and over his kingdom, establishing and upholding it with justice and righteousness from that time on and for ever. The zeal of the Lord Almighty will accomplish this (Isaiah 9:6–7).

Nothing great was or will ever be accomplished without a godly enthusiasm and zeal. Enthusiasm can be cultivated. Enthusiasm makes ordinary people extraordinary. You can make a difference. Edward Hale said:

> I am only one, but I *am* one. I can't do everything, but I *can* do something. And what I *can* do, that I ought to do. And what I *ought* to do, by the grace of God, I *shall* do.[2]

You are a key

Barnabas opened doors for Paul. Barnabas means 'Son of Encouragement'. Although Paul was dramatically converted,

the early church still did not trust him. After all, Paul had persecuted them. This is what happened when Paul tried to be
accepted by the church in Jerusalem:

> When he came to Jerusalem, he tried to join the disciples, but they
> were all afraid of him, not believing that he really was a disciple.
> But Barnabas took him and brought him to the apostles. He told
> them how Saul on his journey had seen the Lord and that the Lord
> had spoken to him, and how in Damascus he had preached fear-
> lessly in the name of Jesus (Acts 9:26–27).

Barnabas took Paul to the apostles and explained his conversion experience and that he was now preaching Jesus as the
Christ, the Son of God. They knew and respected Barnabas
and believed what he said of Paul, and therefore accepted Paul
as well. Barnabas was the key who opened the door for Paul.

Be a blessing and open doors for others.

Doors have opened for me through the Lord's people. Doors
into Africa and Europe have been opened through those who
knew me. Dozens of doors, for work in Britain and overseas,
have been opened for me by my friend J. John. Korky Davey has
opened doors for me in Greece and Nigeria.

We can open doors of blessing and opportunity for others.
Be a blessing and open doors for others. Opening doors can be
exciting. Opening doors can be ordinary. You may not be able
to do a certain thing, but you can enable someone else to do it.
You may not be able to go and preach overseas, but you can give
a financial gift to help someone else go instead. In return for
opening doors for others you will receive the Lord's joy.

You are a key to opening doors. Obedience, confidence, and
enthusiasm are also keys to opening doors. You can succeed.

Never belittle yourself or what you can accomplish. If we can
do big things let us do them, but we can all do little things. Let
us do the little things well. Remember that there is value in little
things.

If I cannot do great things, I can do small things in a great way (J. F. Clarke).[3]

Notes

1. Taken from *Quotes and Anecdotes for Preachers & Teachers* compiled by Anthony P. Castle (Kevin Mayhew Publishers), pages 33–34.
2. Taken from *Courage & Confidence* by Norman Vincent Peale (Cedar), pages 122–123.
3. Taken from *Quotes & Anecdotes for Preachers & Teachers* compiled by Anthony P. Castle (Kevin Mayhew Publishers), page 378.

9.

TOWARDS SPIRITUAL MATURITY

Doctors are helped by the use of X-ray machines.. These machines emit invisible electronic radiation of short wavelengths that pass through the human body. The X-ray pictures show bones, organs and any abnormalities. By taking an inside look at our bodies doctors are able to make a correct diagnosis and to suggest suitable treatment.

God also takes a look at the condition of our hearts. God searches and sees our innermost being. Allowing God to X-ray and search our hearts, motives and desires can lead to significant change. Real change requires an inside look. God can and will reveal our true state if we ask him.

David prayed:

Search me, O God, and know my heart; test me and know my anxious thoughts. See if there is any offensive way in me, and lead me in the way everlasting (Psalm 139:23–24).

David was concerned to know the state of his heart. He asked God to show him. David was also concerned about his thoughts and asked God to test him. Were David's thoughts good, bad or ugly? David did not want to deceive himself. He wanted to know the true condition of his heart. Sin in the heart was David's concern. This was exploratory surgery for sin.

David needed God's help. He did not know if there was any offensive way in his heart. That is why he prayed, 'See if there is any offensive way in me and lead me . . .'

David showed enormous spirituality and humility. He was open to what God would reveal to him.

It is too easy to assume that all is well with the condition of our hearts. I have not met anyone with a perfect heart. Have you? Sin in the heart must be uncovered, looked at and dealt with. An inside look that causes real change is unnerving and so it should be. The diagnosis of sin is not a pleasant experience. We tend to resist whenever we can, preferring to think we have come further than we have. We simply must get to the core of the matter. The kind of change that most delights our Lord will never occur if we deal only with sin in behaviour or obvious sin, neglecting the sin of the heart. Let us examine sin in behaviour and sin in the heart.

The sin of behaviour and the sin of the heart

Sin in behaviour is obvious. Premarital sex, cheating on your wife or husband, physical or sexual abuse, being racist, taking drugs, stealing, being dishonest, reading pornographic magazines, watching pornographic films – these are just a few obvious sins. These sins involve an outward expression and are easily spotted. These matters are clear-cut. These obvious sins can easily be talked about and preached about. It is sin of behaviour that the church has concentrated on. Countless books have been written on these issues, and Christians have rightly been warned about them. In the minds of Christians, when they think about sin, it is usually to do with the sin in behaviour.

Sin of the heart is when we compromise an opportunity to love or do something, in order to stay safe.

If there is to be real change in our lives we must not only concentrate on sin of behaviour. We must look at the sin of the heart, which is just as serious, if not more so.

Jesus warned the teachers of the law and the Pharisees, calling them hypocrites. Although they gave a tenth of their herbs, they had neglected the more important matters of God's law – justice, mercy and faithfulness. Jesus did not say that tithing was unnecessary or unimportant. But he did say that justice, mercy and faithfulness were more important. Jesus said to them:

> 'How terrible for you, teachers of the Law and Pharisees! You hypocrites! You give to God a tenth even of the seasoning herbs, such as mint, dill, and cumin, but you neglect to obey the really important teachings of the Law, such as justice and mercy and honesty. These you should practise, without neglecting the others. Blind guides! You strain a fly out of your drink, but swallow a camel!' (Matthew 23:23–24, Good News Bible).

On the outside the Pharisees and teachers of the law were respectable, good and clean. But on the inside their hearts were full of greed and self-indulgence (Matthew 23:25–26). Jesus told them to first clean the inside and then the outside would also be clean. Jesus was concerned with the state of people's hearts.

Exposing sin of the heart is no easy matter. When justice, mercy and faithfulness are thrown out or neglected it is a sin of the heart. Sin of the heart is when we have sacrificed someone's feelings in order to build our own self-image. Often the result is that people are crushed underfoot. Sin of the heart is when we compromise an opportunity to love or do something, in order to stay safe. These sins are much more difficult to recognise. Even when we do recognise the offence, we do not always call it sin. Sin of the heart often goes unnoticed. The problem in the heart is far worse than many suppose.

Changing our hearts

God can help us change. He can change our heart. God changes our heart through his Spirit, his word and his people. Allow the searching, illuminating light of God in your life.

Search me . . . and know my heart . . . see if there is any offensive way in me . . . (Psalm 139:23–24).

The heart can be desperately wicked. We can easily fool ourselves that all is well, when it is not. Allowing God to search us is not as easy as it sounds. It can be difficult and painful to give Jesus free access to search our hearts. This is an uncomfortable process, but essential for growth.

The Holy Spirit convicts us of our sin (John 16:8). This searching does not take place in a moment. It is a continuous process throughout our lives. We must allow our souls to find rest before God. Life can be fast and busy. Our minds are often occupied with many things. Be still before God. It is vital to find time to be alone with God. The Holy Spirit can search us best when we are quiet and still. Walk with God. Talk with God. Sense him speaking to you. Feel the searching work of the Holy Spirit.

More things happen when God talks to us than at any other time. We have traditionally placed great emphasis on one aspect of prayer: us talking. For us to advance with God, he must speak to us. Let him speak to you. Listen to him.

One of the things I like to do is to get in the car and go to my favourite quiet spot. There I spend a few hours with God. Often I find that during the first hour I am experiencing rest in my soul. During the next hour I read some scriptures and think deeply about them. The third hour I commune with God. It is in that kind of environment that the Spirit of God is able to search me.

The word of God can also search our hearts. Allow the words and promises to touch your heart. We need to be real here. Apply the word of God to your situation and allow your mind to be touched by the truth from the Bible. Let the word do its work.

All Scripture is God-breathed and is useful for teaching, rebuking, correcting and training in righteousness, so that the man of God may be thoroughly equipped for every good work (2 Timothy 3:16–17).

The purpose of God's word is clearly stated: 'so that the man of God may be thoroughly equipped'. Whoever we are, wherever we live, God's word is relevant. God's word instructs and shows the way forward, the way to progress and succeed. Most importantly it shows us how to have good hearts.

God's word speaks and changes our hearts when we allow it to. There is something in God's word that is useful for every situation that we may face. Jesus spoke about murder, adultery, divorce, making promises, loving enemies, giving to the needy, prayer, treasures in heaven, being anxious, judging others, persevering in prayer and in life (Matthew 5–7).

Growth sometimes requires discomfort.

It is one thing to know God's word. But it is another thing to put it into action. It can be difficult to allow God to touch our hearts, especially if we suspect that we need rebuking or correcting. I have known few people who have been joyful when God has rebuked or corrected them!

Another way our hearts can change is through God's people. Christians can try to wriggle out of a difficult situation. We try to avoid being rebuked or corrected, especially through another person. Growth sometimes requires discomfort. It may be through long-term friendships or even a chance meeting with someone. As a result our lives are enriched and our hearts can be changed. We may find the situation changes for the better. God can change our hearts. Your heart can change while listening to a speaker, when having coffee with a friend, through reading, listening to a tape, or while watching a video. Change can occur through a counsellor. Change can occur through a planned event. It may come suddenly and unexpectedly. We should be open and relaxed.

But be warned: sometimes a well-meaning person, even a leader, can do great damage by bad advice or suggestions. Damage can be done whether the advice is acted upon or not. Christians in leadership positions have a privileged responsibility to be good shepherds. I have known leaders cause destruction by their inappropriate actions and words, even though they sounded good and godly at the time. Words said to us, especially those words that give direction, must be tested. We should test them with God's word and share them with trusted friends. Jesus said:

> 'But if anyone causes one of these little ones who believe in me to sin, it would be better for him to have a large millstone hung around his neck and to be drowned in the depths of the sea. Woe to the world because of the things that cause people to sin! Such things must come, but woe to the man through whom they come!' (Matthew 18:6–7).

God changes our hearts. He helps us change by searching us through his word and his people. He can and will change us only if we are willing for him to do so.

Don't stay content as you are. Become fully the person God wants you to be and move towards spiritual maturity.

10.

WHAT THE WORLD NEEDS

Love. Everyone wants to be loved. What is it? Love calls out to others, meets the deepest needs in others, brings freedom; love calms the storms of life, heals, provides; love listens to the truth and is willing to change; love rebukes, destroys the work of evil, welcomes all; love demonstrates righteous anger, has integrity; love foresees the future and says, 'Be careful'; love sacrifices; love is willing to die and love wins through in the end.

The dictionary defines character as the collective qualities (especially mental and moral) that distinguish a person or thing. The loving character of Jesus is shown by Mark, the first-century gospel writer. Jesus was characterised by love that knew no limits. What was he like? What kind of love was it? Jesus was patient and kind. He was not jealous or conceited or proud. He was not ill-mannered, selfish or irritable. Jesus did not keep a record of wrongs. He was not happy with evil but was happy with the truth. Jesus never gave up. He had faith, hope and love for others and himself.

Love calls

As Jesus walked along the seashore of Lake Galilee he saw two fishermen. One was Simon, the other his brother Andrew. They were busy catching fish with a net.

'Come follow me,' Jesus said, 'and I will make you fishers of men.'

86

Immediately the two brothers left their nets and went with Jesus. Love calls, believes and makes you into someone different and better. Jesus called the first disciples to become fishers of men (Mark 1:16–18).

Love meets the deepest needs

The house where Jesus was teaching was full of people. The crowd overflowed outside. The paralysed man was lowered down through the roof in front of Jesus. Everyone could see the man's problem. It was obvious that he was paralysed. However the man had a deeper need. It was for forgiveness. Jesus saw this need and said to him, 'Son, your sins are forgiven' (Mark 2:1–12)

Then he healed him. Jesus meets the deepest needs. Jesus forgives.

Love appoints and sets free

Jesus went up a mountain and called to himself those he wanted. The twelve disciples came to him. Jesus appointed and designated them apostles. They would be with him and he would send them out to preach. Jesus gave them the authority to drive out demons (Mark 3:13–19). Love appoints, and sets free to do good to others. Jesus appointed and designated apostles.

Love calms a storm

Jesus got into a boat with his disciples. Suddenly a furious, violent wind arose. The waves began to flood the boat. Jesus was at the back of the boat sleeping with his head on a pillow. His disciples woke him. They asked him if he cared that they were about to die. Jesus got up and spoke to the wind and the waves, commanding them to be still. The wind died down. There was a great calm. Love calms a storm. Jesus saved the disciples from drowning (Mark 4:35–41).

Love heals

The incident where Jesus raises to life the daughter of Jairus and heals the sick woman is perhaps one of the most moving and loving gospel stories.

A synagogue ruler by the name of Jairus approached Jesus with faith and respect. He asked Jesus to save his dying daughter. Jairus fell at Jesus' feet and pleaded earnestly with him: 'My little daughter is dying. Please come and put your hands on her so that she will be healed and live.'

Jesus went with Jairus. On the way Jesus was confronted by a woman who had suffered from bleeding for twelve years. She touched Jesus' garment and was immediately healed. Jesus stopped to affirm and confirm her faith publicly.

He continued his journey to Jairus's home only to find that the girl had died. This was not a problem. Jesus raised her to life. The girl stood up and walked around. She was just twelve years old. Everyone was amazed. Love heals. Jesus healed the daughter of Jairus and the sick woman (Mark 5:21–43).

Love provides

Jesus was faced with a large crowd of hungry people. His disciples wanted to send them away to buy some food. Jesus was not impressed with this suggestion and intervened. Taking a few loaves and fish, he prayed to his Father. The food miraculously multiplied. The 5,000 men, plus women and children, were fed. Love provides. Jesus fed the hungry. To the disciples he said, 'You give them something to eat' (Mark 6:37).

> Christians alone straddle the whole spectrum of rich nations and therefore Christians can be a lobby of tremendous importance. When we come before our heavenly Father and he says, 'Did you feed them, did you give them something to drink, did you clothe them, did you shelter them?' and we say, 'Sorry, Lord, but we did give them 0.3 per cent of our gross national product.' I don't think that will be enough (Barbara Ward).[1]

Love listens to the truth and adjusts

Jesus went to the territory near to the city of Tyre where he went into a house. A Greek woman came and begged Jesus to deliver her daughter from evil (Mark 7:24–30).

> 'First let the children eat all they want,' he told her, 'for it is not right to take the children's bread and toss it to their dogs.'

In other words Jesus said, 'No.' But the woman did not give up: 'Yes, Lord,' she replied, 'but even the dogs under the table eat the children's crumbs.'

Jesus listened and replied: 'For such a reply, you may go; the demon has left your daughter.'

Love listens to the truth and adjusts. Jesus listened to the woman and changed his mind. On returning home the Greek woman found her daughter well and the demon gone.

Love rebukes

The disciples, especially Peter, often got it wrong. Peter did not approve when Jesus spoke to him of the suffering, rejection and death he was soon to encounter (Mark 8:31–33). Peter took Jesus aside and told him off for saying these things. Jesus turned and looked at his disciple and rebuked him: 'Out of my sight, Satan!' he said. 'You do not have in mind the things of God, but the things of men.'

Love rebukes. Jesus rebuked Peter.

Love destroys the work of Satan

A man brought his son to Jesus asking him for help (Mark 9:17–27). The boy could not hear or speak. Often his life was in danger because he would fall into water or fire. Jesus commanded the evil spirits that had hindered the boy's well-being to come out of him and never to enter him again. The boy shook. Jesus took him by the hand and he stood up. He was well. Love destroys the work of Satan. Jesus delivered a boy from evil spirits. The Son of God appeared for this very reason, to destroy the work of the devil (1 John 3:8).

Love welcomes all

People brought children to Jesus for him to place his hands on them and bless them (Mark 10:13–16). The disciples wrongly rebuked the people. When Jesus saw this he was angry and rebuked his disciples saying, 'Let the little children come to me, and do not hinder them, for the kingdom of God belongs to such as these.'

Jesus welcomed these children. He took them in his arms and placed his hands on each of them, blessing them again and again. Love welcomes all. Jesus welcomes all people, whatever age, colour or background.

Love demonstrates righteous anger

On reaching Jerusalem Jesus came to the temple area (Mark 11:15–19). This area was the only part of the temple in which the Gentiles could worship God and gather for prayer. The area that was reserved for Gentiles was occupied with tables, money changers and animal pens. The court of the Gentiles became a noisy, smelly market place. The Jewish religious leaders were interfering with the provision that God had given to the Gentiles. Jesus made a whip out of cords (John 2:15) and used it to drive all from that place, including sheep and cattle. He overturned the tables of the money changers, scattering coins everywhere. He allowed no one to carry any goods through. 'Stop!' Jesus told the people. 'Is it not written: "My house will be called a house of prayer for all nations"? But you have made it "a den of robbers".'

The whole crowd was amazed at his teaching. The chief

priests and teachers of the law were afraid of him and began looking for ways to kill him.

They knew he was absolutely right. Jesus knew that his action would infuriate them. He was not afraid of their feelings because he was at home with his own feelings. Jesus is more often thought of in terms of his compassion, gentleness and restraint; but he knew the whole range of emotions, some of them very passionate and disturbing. Jesus' response to the injustice in the temple was righteous.

In his book *Anger: What to do about it* Richard Walters writes:

> Indignation is the proper reaction to injustice if it energises our physical and emotional systems to oppose evil, to right the wrongs that have been done to those we care about, and to work hard for social changes that will spare others from abuse and suffering. Feelings of anger can spring out of a Christian's sensitivity to human welfare. While rage and resentment are aggressive, seeking to destroy their target, indignation seeks to mobilise the forces of good to challenge and defeat the forces of destruction and oppression.[2]

Love demonstrates righteous anger. Jesus cleared the temple displaying his anger and bringing justice; that was love.

Love has integrity

Some Pharisees and Herodians came to Jesus commenting on his moral excellence:

> 'Teacher, we know you are a man of integrity. You aren't swayed by men, because you pay no attention to who they are; but you teach the way of God in accordance with the truth' (Mark 12:13–14).

They were correct about Jesus' integrity but they had a hidden agenda and wanted to catch him out. Jesus was honest, sound, right, transparent; what you saw of him in public was true in private. Love has integrity. Jesus demonstrated this quality throughout his life.

Love foresees, warns and says, 'Be careful'

Sitting on the Mount of Olives, opposite the temple, Jesus spoke to Peter, James, John and Andrew about the future (Mark 13:5–12, 23). He foresaw what would happen concerning the world. He spoke to them about wars, nations fighting one another, earthquakes multiplying, and future famines. Jesus told them what would happen to them personally. He warned them and told them to watch their step. Love foresees, warns and says, 'Be careful.'

David Wilkerson, the American evangelist, one day foresaw something going wrong in the life of the evangelist Jimmy Swaggart. Wilkerson told Swaggart 'to separate himself – to go to the desert'[3] and to be careful. Unfortunately Swaggart did not listen to the warning and was not careful. He committed adultery with a prostitute. Although these events occurred in America the news appeared on national British television. Television news showed Jimmy Swaggart apologising for his behaviour. I am afraid it was too late. Now he would have to live with the consequences. Jesus warns and at times says, 'Be careful.' Are we listening? Allow his Spirit to speak to you about your life. Allow his Spirit to speak through you to others.

Love sacrifices

In the Garden of Gethsemane on Thursday evening, a few hours before that horrific crucifixion, Jesus experienced physical and mental torture. He was arrested by the religious leaders, severely beaten and spat on. Jesus became a sacrifice to save humanity. Love sacrifices. In the Garden Jesus was almost overwhelmed to the point of death (Mark 14:32–34). This is sacrificial love.

Love is willing to die

The greatest demonstration of love is for a person to give their life for another. Jesus said:

> 'Greater love has no-one than this, that one lay down his life for his friends' (John 15:13).

Jesus allowed himself to be taken, flogged and crucified because of his great love for humanity (Mark 15). His death and shed blood bring forgiveness and new life today for all who repent, believe and receive new birth by the Holy Spirit. Jesus' death proved and showed his love for us. Love is willing to die. Jesus was crucified to death. That is love.

Love wins

Love never fails. In the end love will win through. Having killed Jesus his enemies thought that would be the end of him. Death could not hold Jesus. Jesus was resurrected (Mark 16:1–8). Love wins through. Jesus is risen!

Notes

1. Taken from *Quotes & Anecdotes for Preachers & Teachers* compiled by Anthony P. Castle (Kevin Mayhew Publishers), page 68.
2. Taken from *Anger: What to do about it* by Richard P. Walters (IVP), page 11.
3. Taken from *David Wilkerson: A Final Warning* by Nicky Cruz (New Leaf Press), page 110.

ABOUT THE AUTHOR

Andy Economides' work and passion is to spread the Good News of Jesus and bring people to know and follow Christ, throughout the UK and in other countries. Particular emphasis is given to the nurture of new believers and the training of leaders and churches. Andy is Patron of Prospect College and School, Nigeria, West Africa. Through his fund-raising a new school has been established and the college extended. Scholarships for college students and sponsorships for children are provided through Soteria Trust.

Andy originally qualified as an engineer and worked for six years in research and development. For ten years he was on the staff of a church as a lay minister and evangelist. In 1989 St John's Theological College, Nottingham, awarded Andy the College Hood for Theological and Pastoral Studies. In 1994 Andy became founder and director of Soteria Trust, a registered charity. The word *Soteria* is Greek for 'salvation'. He was ordained a Christian minister in 1998.

If you would like to know more about the ministry of Andy Economides through Soteria Trust, or would like to order books and resources, please complete the response slip and send it to:

Soteria Trust
P.O. Box 103
Chichester
West Sussex, PO19 2XY
UK

Telephone: 01243 771494
Fax: 01243 771240
E-mail: admin@soteriatrust.org.uk
Website: www.soteriatrust.org.uk

Registered Charity No. 1040766

RESPONSE SLIP

Please send me

- ❏ The *Soteria News* regularly
- ❏ Information about books and tapes available
- ❏ Information about how I can be involved

I enclose a gift of £.............. towards the ministry of Soteria Trust. (Please make all cheques payable to *Soteria Trust*.)

Name ....

Address ....

.... Postcode ....

E-mail ....